A Celebration of Poets

A Celebration
of Poets

EDITED AND WITH

AN INTRODUCTION BY

Don Cameron Allen

THE JOHNS HOPKINS PRESS: BALTIMORE

90952

This book was originally published as FOUR POETS ON POETRY and
THE MOMENT OF POETRY, in 1959 and 1962, respectively.
Second printing, 1967

Johns Hopkins Paperbacks edition, 1967

Preface

THOSE OF US WHO BELIEVE THAT poetry is a form of knowledge and that the poet's mode of thinking is a valid means of understanding the mortal world, where what is called "rational agreement" is simply agreement, have always found of extraordinary importance the comments of poets on themselves, on other poets, and on poetry. It is, indeed, pleasant to discover how acceptable this conclusion has become in the world of learning. Most American colleges and universities now assume that the actual presence of the artist's living imagination is as essential to their intellectual life—and hence to that of the nation—as the scholar's discriminating memory and the scientist's mathematical logic. Unlike most of their European counterparts, few distinguished American places of higher learning welcome and honor the academician with no skill in either words or colors, who discourses on literature and art, and exclude the true man of letters or art. Poets of reputation and achievement are now the cherished inhabitants of many American campuses. Here they are not required, as sometimes they are abroad, to hide their talents under the mask of a scientist

v

or scholar; they may follow their proper bents by cultivating their own artistic powers and by bringing to fruition the talents of younger people. Though not an unknown custom in the last century when few American poets went in want, the happy admission of the poet to the university faculty is one of the more noble aspects of our contemporary culture.

The Johns Hopkins University, which named the poet Sidney Lanier to its first faculty, has always subscribed to the doctrine that poetry is a way of seeking the truth that sets men free. In November, 1958, and October, 1961, it brought to its halls two groups of distinguished poets whose talks I am honored to publish in this volume. The late R. P. Blackmur of Princeton University explicates with his usual accurate sensitivity the poetry of the fine English poet Edwin Muir; and Yvor Winters, who has taught and sponsored so many fine young poets, looks backward to the Renaissance and marks some major distinctions in the artistic manner of that age. Marianne Moore, who is not only one of the world's finest poets but also has become through her visits to so many campuses a kind of professor general, gives generous tribute to the writings of the late Dame Edith Sitwell. Mark Van Doren, now retired as Professor of English at Columbia, writes about Thomas Hardy, whose books have been his lifelong companions. John Holmes, late teacher of English at Tufts College and author of many books of verse and books about verse, describes, by expanding his metaphor of Stonehenge, the poet's milieu, the things that stand round the poet and make him poet. Miss May Sarton, author since 1938 of six books of verse and seven novels, modestly disavows her critical powers and then proceeds to tell us, as she has often told her students at Wellesley College, how a poet works. Richard Eberhart, Professor of English at Dartmouth, whose *Collected Poems, 1930-1960* have recently been published, distinguishes between two aspects of poetic thought which he defines as "will" and "psyche." All of these poets talk about other poets, but the poets Randall Jarrell and Richard Wilbur center their critical imaginations on definite poems. Mr. Wilbur, Professor of English at Connecticut Wesleyan and the most brilliant poet of the new generation, shows us that we require more than naked wit to understand what seems at first a simple lyric satire. In the like vein, the late Randall Jarrell, Professor at the Woman's College of the University of North Carolina, novelist, and translator, whose *Woman at the Washington Zoo* won the National Book Award, shows us how to find our way through the not immediately visible artistic complications of one of Robert Frost's great poems.

We can only hope that these essays will find as many enthusiastic readers as they had hearers. But they can hardly go forth without the editor acknowledging the help that made them possible. First, he should like to thank the members of the Turnbull family of Baltimore whose gift in memory of a talented man, Percy Graeme Turnbull, endowed these lectures, the Turnbull Memorial Lectures. Next, he is extremely thankful to the Bollingen Foundation of New York City, whose generous grants made both Johns Hopkins Poetry Festivals possible.

DON CAMERON ALLEN

BALTIMORE, 1967

Contents

A Celebration of Poets

Don Cameron Allen

Introduction

IN ITS BRIGHTER AND HIGHER aspects the purpose of all human thinking is the capture of a greatly desired but agilely elusive substance called truth. The nature of this substance, or perhaps it is only a quality, is grievous to define, and for this reason its pursuit is difficult. Philosophers, on whom we depend for our knowledge of abstractions, have exerted themselves beyond measure to lock whatever they have felt or half-known about truth into the steel cell of a comprehensive and endurable statement. Sometimes they will say that truth is the apparent correspondence of an intellectual proposition to reality; sometimes they will say just the opposite. Theologians tell us that truth is a matter of revelation, but empiricists inform us, then, that there is no implement labeled revelation in the cabinet of knowledge.

In a more honest and less complex age than ours, truth was often measured by the *consensus gentium*. Whatever was accepted by the majority of peoples in most places through a great deal of time was assumed to be true. This was a good doctrine for men of more naïve but happier generations, but more than three hundred years ago it began to lose respect. The genial Montaigne, who lived during the sixteenth century, was shocked to discover how different and contradictory were human notions about matters that cultivated Europeans thought innately understood. In the centuries since Montaigne's death the situation has not improved; nevertheless, there is something in the heart of man that impels him to seek the face of truth although it is likely to be a face veiled or distorted by grimace. Hence, though we cannot define truth, we pursue it; and though the quarry is very much like a phantom fox fleeing through a foggy meadow, we have, good huntsmen that we are, attempted to establish some rules of the chase. We know the laws of the field and the forest even though we do not know what we hunt.

In the same age in which Montaigne was weaving the fabric of doubt and urging men to try truth by the paradox, Sir Philip Sidney took up the challenge of the anti-poets—the challenge invented by the poet Plato—and attempted to defend poetry as a form of thinking and a means to truth. He had the good sense to base his *Apologie for Poetrie* on supra-empirical arguments and to select his best weapons from the armory of the anti-poets. What he wrote was actually a lawyer's brief, and he opens his case by pleading that poetry requires no defense because it is all a matter of taste. It is something we like or dislike, and nothing can really be done about it. But having spoken as an advocate with full attention to the rites of forensic practice, he concludes, when he has reached the tail of his defense, as a theologian, inviting us to believe in revelation.

> *Believe* that [poets] were the first bringers-in of all civility . . . *believe* . . . that no philosopher's precepts can sooner make you honest than the reading of Vergil; . . . *believe* . . . that it pleased the Heavenly Deity . . . under the veil of

fables to give us all knowledge, logic, rhetoric, philosophy, natural and moral, and *quid non*; . . . *believe* . . . that there are many mysteries contained in poetry, which of purpose were written darkly lest by profane wits it should be abused; . . . *believe* that they are so beloved of the gods that whatsoever they write proceeds of a divine fury.

For Sidney, as for some critics and poets who succeeded him, poetry is a kind of religion. He would probably have said that an anti-poet could not be a religious man. He also realized that poetry must be believed tantamount to revelation, and he held for this reason that it was superior as a mode of thought and a form of knowledge to both history and philosophy. I should hardly want to go so far as Sidney and set up an evaluative hierarchy because such an attempt would be not only perilous but, in this late age, vain. However, the poet of *Astrophel and Stella* has made a pattern for me; and after adding science and scientific thinking to his list of intellectual disciplines, I should like eventually to consider poetry as a means of thought and as a repository of knowledge.

When Thucydides, the father of history, sat down to write his account of the Peloponnesian War, he was so conscious of the novelty of the undertaking that he felt called upon to explain what he was doing. "My conclusions," he said, "are drawn from proofs that may safely be relied on. Assuredly they will not be disturbed either by the lays of a poet displaying the exaggerations of his craft, or by the compositions of chroniclers whose main attraction is their avoidance of truth." There is no question about what is said here. A good historian is a diligent scanner of the appearances of reality who avoids the entanglements of the imagination as incompatible with the due processes of reason. Thucydides and his lineal descendants have generally contented themselves with reporting the facts in spatial contexts and chronological sequences that are agreeable to the unimaginative section of the brain. "If I have used a fine style," says the historian Cassius Dio, fearful that his readers would think him a man of letters, "no one on this account will, I hope, question the truth of the narrative; for I have endeavoured to be exact . . . as far as possible." This fear of literary taint is consonant with the injunctions of Thucydides, and we can well imagine the chagrin of a modern historian whose book was described as "fanciful."

History may certainly be a treasury of knowledge, but the historian thinks by assembling without exaggeration or ornamentation a sequence of dead facts that resemble truth in the past tense. The basic difference between history and poetry or the historian and the poet, as the Greeks made it out, is found in Lucian's *The Way to Write History*. This amiable Syrian of the second century cannot endure what he calls "word painting," and he abominates historians who describe events that never occurred. These types of writing, he complains, are the common habits of poets "although one has always thought that there was some difference between the two arts." I suppose that if we want history, Lucian is right. What we ask of an historian is an accurate account of what happened, or what, according to most witnesses, seemed to happen. If the historian was present at a battle, a coronation, an election, a treaty of peace, or a pact of alliance, we hope that he has made allowance for his personal excitement or psychic state, for the sort of season and time of year, for the smoke of cannon or of oratory, for noise, confusion, point of vantage, and the bad correction in the left lens of his eye-glasses. If he works with documents, as most historians do, we hope that he has evaluated their genuineness, searched out the prejudices of their authors, and smoothed out their distortions. We also trust that he has been able to separate the almost true from the slightly false. The poet, who is attempting our imagination and through it our feelings, who will convince us by metaphor rather than by syllogism, will happily violate all of the historians' rules. He will twist and expand the evidence; he will embrace the testimony of the least reliable and most imaginative witnesses; he will, as Lucian says in his lament over the fanciful historians, "have one man kill seventy at a blow." For the poet is committed by his metaphor to enlargement just as the historian is urged to containment by the fact.

Examples of the distortion of the historical doctrine by poets may be observed whenever a poet selects an historical theme as the subject of his imaginative meditations. When, for instance, Shakespeare wrote *King Lear*, he turned for his preliminary information to a firmly trusted book, the *Histories of the Kings of Britain* by Geoffrey of Monmouth. Here he read of the foolish old king, who had three daughters of whom he loved Cordelia, the youngest, the best. Resolving to divide his kingdom, he proposed a love test in which Cordelia fared badly, but not so badly that she was unacceptable as a dowerless bride to the king of France. Then Lear is treated harshly by the other daughters, flies to France, and is restored by Cordelia's armies to his throne. He rules bravely for three years, dies, and his beloved Cordelia, now a widow, succeeds him. The end is bitter. The sons of the evil sisters rebel; Cordelia is defeated and imprisoned, "wherein," says Geoffrey, "overwhelmed with grief of her lost kingdom, she slew herself." This is the story retold by the British historians and put in rime by some of Shakespeare's lesser contemporaries. The end is always the same;

and for most men of the Elizabethan age, the damp of gloom
rises not from the sufferings of Lear, but from the despair and
suicide of Cordelia. It is the historically accurate but unendurable climax; it violates all the emotions. We ask ourselves,
as Shakespeare must have asked himself, whether the life of
a charming and devoted young woman, who had rescued her
misjudging father, should end in self-destruction.

It is small wonder that Shakespeare was repelled by this
history, for it makes all things awry and fouls his poetic definition of the universe. It was unseemly to him that a girl,
benevolent and forgiving, should yield to the sin of despair, the
sin against the Holy Spirit. Granted that all of this happened
in pre-Christian Britain, the end was too savage; for even the
wild gods of Euripides see to it that the pious and devoted
Iphigenia is preserved. It was unbelievable that Cordelia should
be found in that circle of Hell where suicides are suspended
"each on the thorny tree of its tormented shade." So Shakespeare turns his back on history and makes a minority report.
The battle is lost; Lear never regains the crown; and Cordelia
is murdered in prison by the forces of evil against which Shakespeare eternally protests. It is a new end to history that Lear
himself foresees.

> Upon such sacrifices my Cordelia
> The gods themselves throw incense.

Despair finds no port or entry in the character of Cordelia
as Shakespeare remade her. She is cleansed of her historical
disease, and it is transferred instead to her father and to his
alter ego, the Duke of Gloucester. From the emendable .despair
of these two men, the theme of Shakespeare's tragedy is wrought.
By concentrating on the eating desperation and anger of Lear,

Shakespeare denies the testimony of the historians and invents a new rule by means of which the character of Lear may be construed. The histories say little about this. The king, says Geoffrey, was "grieved beyond measure," and this moderate statement is not inflated by Geoffrey's successors. Even in the anonymous play of *King Leir*, which is Shakespeare's partial model, the despair and remorse of Lear is so tame that we are totally unaffected. Yet it is from this germ of suggestion that Shakespeare, thinking as a poet, begets the titanic passion, the brain-rending misery that besets the aged king. To call forth this passion and this misery, he creates a man whom the historians have never known.

When I observe that poetry and poetical thinking have almost nothing in common with history and historical thinking, I expect that some critics of literature and some historians will agree with me. I am also aware that historians are still urged to use literary texts as documents, which, indeed, they never are; and that some critics will always be busy with the historical background of literature, which is a pleasant but generally unattractive form of non-literary effort. But this type of self-entertainment is probably not so wasteful as that of those critics who hold that poetical thinking is a half-sister to scientific thinking and that poetry is a kind of science. In this age when the sciences have been inclined to adopt in certain of their areas a quasi-imaginative character, this form of speculation is likely to carry a little weight.

The poet, say the proponents of the science of poetry, is as fascinated as the scientist by the inner nature of things and never concerns himself, as the historian does, with external appearances. This is Wordsworth listening to the systole and diastole of nature; this is Browning seated, notebook in hand, at humanity's couch; this is even Milton connected by some sort of fleshly short wave to the council halls of Heaven and Hell. The critics of literature who are dazzled by this illusion are aided and abetted by the agitated outcries of certain theoretical scientists who are engaged in establishing an electronic proof of the existence of God. The fault that mars this hypothesis is that it is neither scientific nor poetic, since it depends on a sort of uncontrolled imagination that is inimical to both science and poetry.

I should be the first to admit that there is some sort of connection between the engendering idea of the poet and what used to be called the "scientific hunch," but it is exactly at this point that all similarities between science and poetry cease. Bitter as the realization may be, we must remember that philosophers—those men who are mainly concerned with areas of knowledge abandoned by the scientists, theologians, psychologists, economists, political theorists, and aestheticians—long ago gave up the search for what was once called inner essence or the-thing-in-itself. When philosophers withdraw from any proposition, it has to be totally impossible as a subject of speculation. No scientist, I think, is likely to assume that there is a difference between appearance and reality; and we can hardly believe that what the scientist has thrown over as a reasonable subject of inquiry, the poet through some special endowment has fruitfully discovered.

In the main, science and poetry, scientific and poetical thinking have almost nothing in common. The scientist is really engaged in averaging external experience into laws. The poet, on the contrary, is ordinarily unimpressed by the average and is principally attracted by uniqueness, by the sort of phenomenon that the scientist calls the variant, the aberration of a fixed order.

But the scientist and the poet are separate in other respects. The scientist is eager, I think, to convey his impressions of the average of appearances in the linguistic cart of non-subjective symbols that will be recognized by his fellow scientists, who will answer him in the same symbols. The poet is not averse to symbols; he is, in fact, trapped by them into his poem; but his notion of symbols is entirely different from that of the scientist. The scientist wants an unambiguous symbol that will mean exactly the same thing to all other scientists. The poet, too, wants his symbols to have meaning, but his are not limited meanings. The poem of his youth may have even for him a different meaning in old age. For his readers—and I am thinking of the informed and sensitive ones—it may have still other meanings. Accuracy is not an end for the poet, and it is not guaranteed by the modes of poetical thought. But there is another difference between the symbolic language of the poet and that of the scientist.

For the scientist the symbol is a means of conveying fact; for the poet it is a way of transmitting emotion. This emotion has no connection with hysteria or with nervous agitation. It is plainly the emotion attendant on a creative act carried through or on the uniqueness of the metaphor that releases the poet from further speculation. Its validity comes from success or relief and sometimes from both. It is at each end of its circuit completely subjective, and in this major respect it is altogether unscientific. A scientist who wishes to tell another scientist about a stone will probably say that it is " a concreted earthy or mineral substance of such-and-such chemical composition." A poet will drop the same stone in a forest pool and describe it with the birdsong evoked by the splash of the water. What the bird sings will tell the poet's readers, as it has told him, all that need be known about the stone, the pool, and the forest. But this is certainly not science, and it is not the way the scientist thinks.

If poetry is not history or science, if the way the poet thinks is not like the way the scientist or the historian think, we may ask ourselves whether or not we find some connection between poetry and philosophy or the poet and the philosopher. Sidney saw a connection, but he thought that the poet's thought was better thought. The poet and the metaphysician share the analogical process, and both poets and philosophers stand outside the material engagements of modern life in a way that is different from the disengagements of the historian and the scientist. When we turn through histories of literature, we come on men who are described as "philosophic poets," although we never find in the histories of philosophy the mention of a "poetical philosopher." The denomination of "philosophical poet" is probably unfortunate; but we have persisted in this unhappy contradiction, and we even write books called *The Philosophy of Milton* or Shakespeare or Shelley when really we mean something else. We are, I suppose, inclined to believe as the ancients were that *poet*, *prophet*, and *philosopher* are synonyms.

The father of philosophy is reported to have said that no sane man knocks on the door of poetry and to have banished poets from his republic; yet Plato, as defenders of poetry have tirelessly pointed out, was something of a poet himself. Then, too, when we read the remains of the philosophers before Socrates we often find expressions that seem to be poetic rather than philosophic. "Nature," writes Heraclitus, "likes to hide." "Victory," says Democritus, "betrays the survivors." Empedocles appears to have the poetical manner when he says, "Stepping from summit to summit, not to travel one path of words to the end," or "the air sank down on the earth with its long roots." This is all usable poetic stuff, but the question does not rest here. Is it philosophy?

If I can assume that prior to Aristotle, philosophers not only thought like poets but were poets, I can be equally sure that since that age they have lost their poetic touch. I am quite ready to agree that there are poetic moments in Bruno, Fichte, and Schopenhauer; Santayana is the most poetical of philosophers and, perhaps, the most philosophical of poets. This is all true, but I also notice that philosophers are most poetical when they are least philosophical. We have, for instance, a fragment of Empedocles which reads, "draining their lives with bronze." Now this may have something to do with the war before Troy, but it might also refer to Greek materialists who were spending themselves in hopes of amassing a fortune. In either case the image is neat and suggestive, and no poet would reject it, but I do not believe that it would gain admittance to the *Journal of Philosophy* in its Empedoclean shape. It would have to be revised to read something like this: "The current inclination towards the dissipation of the life force in the temporality of material contention is one of the principal amoral stimuli of this century." The difference in the two statements is obvious. Empedocles is more stirring, unliteral, non-exact. As in the case of scientific thinking, it is again a question of univalence versus multivalence, or rational thought versus imaginative thought.

In the history of so-called philosophical poetry, only Lucretius and Dante have been eminently successful as poets. Lucretius, who has a mild enough philosophical success to be mentioned in histories of that art, is, as any Latinist knows, a far better poet when he is composing a hymn to Venus or standing in artistic awe before the circle of the stars than when he is mirroring

Epicurus and discussing the *clinamen* of the atoms. Dante succeeds as a philosophical poet because he is not a philosophical poet at all. Had he put the *Summa Theologica* into *terza rima*, he would be unread and probably unknown except to professional mediaevalists. He excels and has his place in the forum of poetry because he exemplified the doctrines of Aquinas; he does not describe or expound them. We understand Dante's aesthetic better if we have read Aquinas; we do not read Dante to comprehend the *Summa*.

Poets are seldom philosophers, and they do not get sealed of this tribe by carrying a philosophical system into verse. Some poets of second- or third-class talent have attempted this metamorphosis into philosopher with no success, which is a way of saying no art. They were the victims, I suppose, of the ancient fallacy that whatever is true is beautiful and that whatever is beautiful is poetic; so they confused poetic truth with philosophic truth without realizing that they had naught in common. A sound philosophical system can never be made poetry by hanging it over with metaphors; abstraction has a quiet beauty of its own but it is not that of poetry. Actually, an idea has poetic value only when it is born in poetic shape. The shape and the idea are inseparable; they cannot be forced on each other.

But philosophy used to concern itself with human conduct, with ethics and morality, and there are still some critics left who like to argue that poetry joins with philosophy in cogitating these matters. They are not so naïve as the old-fashioned explicators who sought for the "moral" in the poem. Now they talk about social criticism and human integration which puts it all on a much higher platform, but the end is about the same. As a consequence of this, I must ask myself whether poetry, since it

is unconcerned with what is philosophically true, is really engaged in considering what is ethically good. Most philosophers
would agree that what they call justice, fidelity, temperance,
liberality, and fortitude are ideal ethical goods which all reasonable men should search out. The opposites of these notions,
they would certainly say, should be avoided by social, even by
solitary, man. But if poets agreed with this, we should be
wanting some rather fine poetry. Out of intemperance, Shakespeare made Falstaff; out of infidelity, Macbeth; out of illiber-
ality, Shylock; out of injustice, Othello. I shall not say that
Shakespeare approved of viciousness, for the contrary is clearly
the truth; but evil played an immense role in his poetical thinking, and it has often been the point of suggestion for other poets
as well. It goes without question that poetry can be made out of
material that lacks the stamp of ethical approval. Moral ugliness
and physical ugliness can both be transformed into intense
artistic attractiveness. A fascinating study could be made, I
expect, of the aesthetic of ugliness just as studies were long ago
made about the morality of immorality.

It must be clear by now that I do not think that philosophical
thinking is like poetical thinking or that philosophy has a firm
engagement with poetry. Poetical thought feeds on metaphors.
They are its heart and center. For history, philosophy, and
science they are dubious adjuncts. Somehow or other the essential difference between these forms of knowledge is here.
Granted that all of these means of truth-seeking share in each
other's rights and sometimes are woven loosely together, the
poetical process of thought seems to me to be more different
from the others than they are among themselves. Euclid alone
may have "looked on beauty bare"; and I should be the last to
question the poetic possibilities of geometry, or the philosophical

experience of reading Milton, or the historical values of the *Iliad*; nonetheless, merely to say this suggests, however, that the dissimilarities between these forms of thought are greater than their dependencies. But if poetical thinking is different and if poetry is wisdom, how do we understand this thought and know this wisdom?

In antiquity it was doubted whether poets thought at all. The *Odyssey* begins with " Tell me, O Muse," and many of the older Greek poets announce that they have been presented with their verse by one or other of the fair, bare ladies who haunt the Castalian springs. The first of the English poets, Caedmon, was said to have been so forlorn of poetry that he left the hall where men were singing in tune to the harp and retreated to the byre where the cattle would not ask him for a song. There an angel, the natural Christian Muse, came to him and told him to sing, inspiring him with the topics of his song, and thus he became the first poet of the Angles and Saxons. This elder notion that the poet is the trumpet of the will of God, a notion that Donne emphasizes in *The Second Anniversary,*

> The purpose and th' authoritie is his;
> Thou art the Proclamation; and I am
> The Trumpet, at whose voyce the people came,

persists even unto this day among primitive peoples. The shaman or seer who recites at tribal functions is thought to be the receptacle of a mysterious power that fills him with its words. He is a sort of savage Milton, who can tell confidently

> Of my Celestial Patroness, who deignes
> Her nightly visitation unimplor'd,
> And dictates to me slumbering, or inspires
> Easie my unpremeditated verse.

The inclination to invoke the Muse or the Holy Spirit gave way during the latter part of the eighteenth century to a tendency on the poet's part to invoke himself. It is only occasionally that a later poet—Hopkins for instance—will admit that his poetry "is given him." There is, I think, in this notion that poetry is intelligential rather than ratiocinative, a partial key to the nature of poetical thought.

Schiller once defined art as a form of play, and Vico, the precursor of the critic Croce, said that poetry is the language of children. Some time ago Auden was asked by someone who ought to have known better why poets wrote poetry. To this absurd question he offered a wise answer: they wrote poetry because it was fun. The word that he used is a word that children have always in their mouths. Now I do not think that Schiller or Vico or Auden would say that poetical thinking is childish and that it is improper for adults to write poetry. What all of these men meant is that poetical thinking is totally different from all other kinds of thinking, and that maybe the child's way of observing the universe and describing it is something like the poet's way. There are, I believe, no child philosophers, although Wordsworth knew some, and this fact gives us Wordsworth's definition of philosophy. I can think of no child historians, and the child scientists I have encountered are more child than scientist. But in some degree, in love of rime and of metaphor, the child makes common ground with the poet. The child's way of seeing his world—uncluttered by adult experience, pretensions, and customary patterns of observation—is similar in its uniqueness and surprise to the way that poets see and record experience.

The English poet Traherne, who drew much of his poetical thought from the recollections of his childhood, comes close to the explanation of this notion of the child's world and the poet's world in several of his poems. It is a world in which there is no difference between *me* and *you*, no boundary between the real and the imaginary, between sleep and waking, between poetical thinking and logical thinking. But it is a world that is lost as maturity teaches distinctions.

> O that my Sight had ever simple been!
> And never faln into a grosser state!
> Then might I evry Object still have seen
>   (As now I see a golden Plate)
> In such an hev'nly Light, as to descry
> In it, or by it, my Felicity.

Traherne had to grow up to say this because in the world of his childhood there could be no poetical thinking. In that world all was poetical. The distinctions between the real and the imaginary, between dreaming and waking, have to be made before poetical thinking can come to being. Perhaps this discrimination does not exist; perhaps in stating it I am guilty of a childlike error; nonetheless, it seems to me that there are no dreams in a world of dreams and no poetry where all is poetry. Alexander Pope is saying something like this when he remarks " that he did not wander in fancy's mazes long / But stoop'd to truth and moralized his song." He knew a frontier when he crossed it. The state of fancy was of a different geographical color for him than the realm of philosophical ethics. By making this distinction he was a poet.

Poetical thinking is dependent on logical thinking for the establishment of these lines of demarcation, but in no other respects is it like logical thought. Poetical thinking makes its own rules according to the temperament and skill of each thinker; it abounds in syllogisms that a logician would call false. On the other hand, the historian, philosopher, and scientist follow fixed modes of thought and dominate the appearances of reality by set logical formulae. When it comes to keeping the law, the true poet is an outlaw. There are no rules that we can master that will make us poets, or if we are poor poets, better poets. We may read poetry incessantly. As so many Aristotles, we may tabulate the methods of poets, compile treatises on metrics, structure, rime, and imagery. We may talk about texture and paradox, tenor and vehicle. We may get all of these discoveries by heart, but none of us will be poets because of it. For all of his effort, Aristotle never got to the heart of Greek poetry let alone making himself or his readers the peers of Homer or Euripides. The reason for all of this ill-success is that, unlike logical thinkers, poets work with material that no man can overcome. They may plan a poem in detailed fashion. They may even work out those carefully reasoned structures that scholars and critics are always finding in poems. But if they cannot illogically discard their plan and break their preconceived structure, they are not poets.

A poet constantly astonishes himself, I think, by violating the rules of logical thought. When I say this, I, as a non-poetical thinker, am leaning on the few facts that I have—the working manuscripts of poets. The thinking poet does not walk down the finely swept path of a formally developed and sequent series of logical postulates. He advances by metaphor, which is a form of leaping. The philosopher, the historian, the scientist move as snails on a slate and leave behind them a glistening trail that we can follow with even an unpracticed eye. The poet moves like a ground squirrel; where he is now gives no promise or assurance of where he will be next. He writes a line. He emends it or strikes it out. He makes additions. He switches terms. He throws a stanza away. We can follow him for a moment. We can sometimes explain a change or a sequence by semantics or allusion or association. Then he expunges and achieves the final, the successful version. Often this version has small connection with the earlier tentations.

So, in a sense, poetical thinking can no more be explained than a poem can be explained. Socrates, we remember, complains on one occasion that poets never answer the question, "What does this poem mean?" Rhetoricians, grammarians, pedants, poetical parasites, as he suggests, are always ready to write explanations of poetry. In this observation history bears him out. The great Greek poets who followed Homer do him the honor of borrowing a fable, a phrase, a metaphor, as if to say, "No one else could do this better." It is not until the time of Pindar that he is mentioned at all, and then the simple expression "his divine epics" is enough. Late in the history of classical letters, a second-class poet, Manilius, makes more of him.

> Greece does not know his country,
> Yet there flowed from him
> A singing river for all later men
> Rich in the goods of one man.

While the poets stood in modest silence before the poet, the non-poets—Theagenes of Rhegium, Metrodorus of Lampsacus, Eustathius, Apollonius Dyscolus, Aristarchus, and many others—were correcting, explaining, understanding. If Homer had lived to have read them, he would have thanked his blindness.

Though poetical thinking is essentially non-logical, and though in its way it is detached from common reality, it is not opposed to reality. There is a division between them, not a difference. The poetical mind is separated from reality only in those moments when it is thinking poetically, in those moments when for

it the imaginary is the real or the real the imaginary. The poet
stands outside of the real in his imagination, but he brings the
real into a contracted kind of individual existence through the
metaphor that fantasy awards him. The reality of the metaphor
can be tested only against other metaphors, and the test is made
certain by the intensity of emotional acquiescence. The critic—
and by that word I mean the logical thinker in the common
sense—is seldom capable of this experience. If he is a non-poet,
as he often is, he would consider it mental confusion, a kind of
controlled schizothymia. He is always able to sever and to keep
totally separate the reason and the imagination, the real and the
imagined. For this reason, critics are sometimes taunted with
being frustrated poets, but as a matter of fact every completely
logical man or simply every man who tries to think logically is
a frustrated poet. In the same manner the poet, who can obviously live for only a fraction of each day in the realm of the
imagination, who can think poetically at only isolated and dis-
crete moments, is a frustrated child. The logician might conclude that the poet lives an imperfect life because he occupies
two planes of thought and is, consequently, two different men.
I cannot deny the logician's right to say this, but it also seems
to me that the poet's relations with what we call reality may
be more complete than those of all other men.

The real is not real to the poet because it is real; it is real
because it is fitting. Poets have always talked about seeing things
as they are, and in earlier times they held mirrors up to nature
and wrote down what was therein reflected. The problem in
these statements is linguistic. *Seeing, are, mirrors, nature,* and
reflected have poetic equivalents that the lexicographers do not
put in their books. *Seeing* is *imagining* and some form of this
word governs the definition of all these terms, but none of them

predicates a disregard for the facts of reality. The poetical thinker sees the facts of reality as they are; that is, he sees them out of context. The logical thinkers—historians, philosophers, and scientists—are far less realistic than poets in that they invariably attempt to supply a context which at heart they know does not exist.

One of the gravest tasks of the poet is, consequently, to write a continuous nervous commentary on the thinking of all the non-poets. He must always labor to preserve the fragments of reality in their familiar form in order to keep them from being dissolved into the nothingness, which is a way of saying the rigid systematization, of logical sequences. In other words, the poet once again sees a world in which, like that of the child, casual connections, formal relationships, whys and wherefores are unknown and unwanted. His eyes are unprejudiced by the categories of analysis. His other senses share in the triumph of his eyes, and his imagination creates a new world. Since each poet lives for a moment in this special world and since each poem is a detached and separate thing shown to us by the poet, poetry has never progressed in the sense that history, philosophy, and science have. We can say Ptolemy, Copernicus, Galileo, Kepler, Newton and each name improves its predecessor; but when we say Homer, Dante, Shakespeare, Milton, Goethe, there is only consonance. Poetry really never grows up, for its very existence depends on a constant renewal of its youth.

By regularly renewing its youth, poetry is able to see each day as if it were the first morning of creation. Because of this constant sense of a newly created world, the poet, too, helps in the creation. Sidney, from whom I chose my text on poetry as a form of faith, makes this point as well, saying that thanks to the divine breath in him, the poet is able to bring forth things

" far surpassing " the works of nature. When he writes this, he is modestly rephrasing the words of the poet-critic Scaliger.

> The poet makes another nature and other outcomes for men's acts, and finally, in the same way, makes himself another God. The other sciences are users of what the maker of them produced; but poetry, when it so splendidly gives the appearance of the things that are and of those that are not, seems not to narrate the events as the historians do, but to produce them as a God.

This statement may strike us as lacking in reverence, but in our fathers' thesaurus of metaphors God was often given the name of poet, and the poet and artist was often compared to God. The authority for the comparison began with a text in Plotinus, but Western man fully believed that the Greek Church confessed that it " believed in God the Father, Poet of Heaven and Earth." The obvious error in translation was not, I think, the result of an inadequate knowledge of Greek. There was a firm desire to mistranslate because men wanted God to be a poet and his creation to be a poem. "Then in forming man," says the Italian, Guarini, " the divine voice of the same divine poet indicated that he was pleased with the work of imitation, saying: 'Let us make man in our own image.'"

The connection between God and his mortal analogy, the poet, is described by Shakespeare in a passage so familiar that few readers have bothered to understand it.

> The poet's eye in a fine frenzy rolling,
> Doth glance from heaven to earth, from earth to heaven
> And as imagination bodies forth
> The forms of things unknown, the poet's pen
> Turns them to shapes and gives to airy nothing
> A local habitation and a name.

Because Duke Theseus of *A Midsummer-Night's Dream* speaks in an apparently derogatory fashion, this speech has long been regarded as a jest at the expense of poets. But we must remember that the whole temper of the play belies everything that critics make the Duke say and that Shakespeare carefully distinguishes between the imagination of the poet, the lunatic, and the lover by assigning to the poet a "fine frenzy" just as Drayton, in praising Marlowe, alludes to his "fine madness." But Shakespeare, I expect, goes beyond this to establish a divine analogy.

The world, said the Renaissance, is a poem that may be read in any order—up and down, down and up, forward and backward, backward and forward. Tasso elaborates on this by describing creation as an infinitely ordered epic, with all its parts bound together by a joyous concordance; "while there is nothing lacking in it, yet there is nothing there that does not serve for necessity of ornament." God, who is capable of unending variety and whose similes are things, ornaments the great poem he has written from top to bottom. This poem of creation Shakespeare says, may be read in all directions by the "rolling eye" of the lesser poet. But the poet, unlike God, has only similes with which to express things, but in compensation, like God, he can bring from "airy nothing" the "forms of things unknown." This is for Shakespeare the necessary equation. The poet is God's metaphor; he can create a new world from the great void.

But the world that the poet creates is not the world in which the laws of the scientist, the historian, or the philosopher flourish. It is not a world of firm assertion, but a world of interrogatory thought, for the poet is always the true questioner of the nature of the world that he makes. In general, he is content to stand before it and ask himself what it is, for his whole art depends on the questions that he frames in the tense moment of poetical thought. He understands, too, that it is the correctness of the questions that really matters. In the world that he creates by preserving its separateness, questions and answers are the same. He knows, too, that the propriety of his questions depends to a large degree on his consciousness of the facts of his non-poetic life. So the poet, like the child, is forever interrogating his universe and forever rejecting the answers that logical thinkers are only too eager to give him. Sensing reality for what it is, he has always known that the answers that man invents are imposed on reality and not contained in it. Truth stands in this and in this alone. So the poet understands that the chase is a false hunt and that man at his best can only construct fitting inquiries about the isolated experiences that he has chosen to call reality. This is the end of poetical thinking and the wisdom that is poetry.

But what I have been saying about the nature of poetical thought has probably no validity at all because I write entirely without poetical experience. I have put myself by my own words in the room of those who attempt some kind of logic and who are excluded thereby from the chambers inhabited by poets. Fortunately, I can be corrected by the remarks of the nine poets whose essays follow.

R. P. Blackmur

Edwin Muir:

between the

Tiger's Paws

YOUNG ENGLISHMEN, WHEN asked how they felt about the poetry of Edwin Muir, answered by and large that they had not troubled to make an opinion about it because it had little relation to the serious venture of poetry at this time. There was an intonation of voice that if prompted to make an opinion, it would be a bad one. Young Americans, when asked, returned a restive blankness, rather like the puppy who does not understand what is wanted, and the Americans, in this case, were nearer right than the English if only because they had nothing at all to go on, and the Englishmen (so we like to think) ought to have known better as a race of people given to the making of verse: of making something into verse; a habit which has occasionally produced poetry. I would say that the Americans needed instruction, while the English needed correction about matters of fact. There is something wrong about habits of writing and reading poetry which insist on valuing highly only the professional poetry which springs (when it does not merely make a bog) from those habits.

24

The professional poet and his poetry should be seen as the collapsing chimaeras they mainly, and of necessity, are; then we could scratch where we itch. Then, too, we could enjoy for the hard and interesting things *they* are the verses made by quite unprofessional poets like Edwin Muir out of honest and endless effort and the general materials of their language. In this case, most of us who write would even appreciate ourselves better and would do better what we did and would above all appreciate better the true great poet and how he differs from us only, and enormously, in degree. "*Onorate l'altissimo poeta; l'ombra sua torna, ch'era dipartita.*" Your small poet shares in that honor.

It is only degree. Think of Edwin Muir and listen to these words. "Through all [these images] there runs a feeling, a feeling which is our own no less than the poet's, a human feeling of bitter memories, of shuddering horror, of melancholy, of homesickness, of tenderness, of a kind of childish *pietás* that could prompt this vain revival of things perished, these playthings fashioned by a religious devotion . . . ." No words could better be applied to the praise of Edwin Muir than these; I would alter nothing and add very little, as the remainder of these remarks, of which they will form the burden, will show. But the words were not written about Muir but about a passage in the *Aeneid* to exemplify the complex of images and the spirit which animates them which inhabit all poetry, and they were written [in the *Encyclopedia Britannica*, article "Aesthetics"] by Benedetto Croce. They touch on the point of projection where Muir and Virgil join in kind however distant they may be in degree.

Virgil wrote the will of the Roman Empire when that empire was young. Muir, sturdy in his own way, has written an individual, a personal—an English, a Scotch—footnote to life in the

true empire at a time when the notion of a good empire seems
no longer plausible or possible but only an image for longing
without hope. There is nothing either official or evangelical or
prophetic about him, and least of all is there any plea for the
kind of greatness we call grandeur, public or private. There is,
rather, all Virgil's piety—the childish *pietás*, as Croce puts it—
directed inwards upon the force of his own mind and thence
outwards upon the nature—the naturalist's nature and human
nature—that has affected him. Piety is that medium of conduct
in which we feel and then achieve a harmony in the clashing of
necessities: that harmony which I find myself calling over and
over the concert of conflicts, and which is so difficult to achieve
without the mediating presence of some form of empire, Roman
or not. This difficulty in achieving harmony indeed seems the
characteristic difficulty of the human condition in our times, and
it sometimes seems possible only to think it in verse.

To say that this is what Muir has done is another way of
saying something about the attractive force of Muir's verse: he
has made his harmony in the thought—not the numbers, the
thought—of his verse. Verse for him is the mode of his thoughtful piety, the mode of the mind's action, where his piety is not
only enacted for him but takes independent action on its own
account and for us: when it does, it becomes poetry. This differs
from the usual run of things. Usually, poetry gets along very
well only reflecting thought already entertained or so to speak
without any primary thought at all. I do not say that Muir's
mode is any better, only that it is worth distinguishing how it is
different from, say, the poetry of Ezra Pound or that of Pope.
Pound's thought is in his cadence and numbers; Pope's versifi-
cation cuts off the roots of his thought; Muir's thought is in the
verse itself—hence the sense in the most regular of his verses of

a continuous vital irregularity, whereby we know how alien and independent is thought that has taken on its identity, and how full of war any harmony is in its incarnations.

There is a passage in the chapter on Rome in Muir's auto-biography which bears on the point. It is not, of course, verse, and rings in the "other harmony" of prose. But it leads of a certainty towards poetry, purely and without infection; which is one reason I quote it, with the second reason that my own sense of Rome is in good part Muir's and that in his language he has discovered for me a grand version of the experience I stood con-victed of in Rome. I refer to the current of thought which he communicates in the word *Incarnation*. Rome is where all man-ner of things take to the grace of the body, body in their meet-ings and body in their conflicts, a concert altogether.

> We saw the usual sights [he says], sometimes enchanted, sometimes disappointed; but it was Rome itself that took us, the riches stored in it, the ages assembled in a tumultuous order, the vistas at street corners where one looked across from one century to another, the innumerable churches, palaces, squares, fountains, monuments, ruins; and the Romans themselves going about their business as if this were the natural and right setting for the life of mankind.

> The history of Rome is drenched in blood and blackened with crime; yet all that seemed to be left now was the peace of memory. As we wandered about the Forum we could not summon up the blood-stained ghosts; they had quite gone, bleached by centuries into a luminous transparency, or evapo-rated into the bright still air. Their works were there, but these cast only the ordinary shadow which everything set up by mankind gathers at its foot. The grass in the courtyard of the Temple of the Vestals seemed to be drenched in peace down to the very root, and it was easy to imagine gods and men still in friendly talk together there.

So far the harmony is easy and no more than sensitive to con-trive. "But," he goes on, "it was the evidence of another In-carnation that met one everywhere and gradually exerted its influence." Here Muir reminds himself of the life neighboring the Scotch churches of his boyhood in the persons of their ministers. "In figures such as these the Word became some-thing more than a word in my childish mind; but nothing told me that Christ was born in the flesh and lived on the earth.

In Rome that image was to be seen everywhere, not only in churches, but on the walls of houses, at cross-roads in the suburbs, in wayside shrines in the parks, and in private rooms. I remember stopping for a long time one day to look at a little plaque on the wall of a house in the Via degli Artisti, representing the Annunciation. An angel and a young girl, their bodies inclined toward each other, their knees bent as if they were overcome by love, 'tutto tremante,' gazed upon each other like Dante's pair; and that representation of a human love so intense that it could not reach farther seemed the perfect earthly symbol of the love that passes understand-ing. . . . That these images should appear everywhere, re-minding everyone of the Incarnation, seemed to me natural and right, just as it was right that my Italian friends should step out frankly into life. This open declaration was to me the very mark of Christianity, distinguishing it from the older religions.

The harmony is harder here since it has to do with how harmonies are come by, with the art of the art, the passion of the passion, the story of the story. It is like—as a direct experi-ence—St. Thomas' definition of allegory where the words signify things which themselves then signify further, yet there remain with us only the primitive words or the plaque on the wall. The allegory which Rome provided for Muir out of the monuments and fountains of human ruins and aspirations, and which he

records in his prose, is a kind of prefiguration of the allegory—
the effort to make things speak further for themselves than our
mere words can signify alone—which he completes in his verse.
I should like to point out that these allegories are not—as so
many of our allegories are nowadays—puzzles or evasions or
deliberate ambiguities or veilings of purpose, and they do not
require interpretation according to anything but the sense of
intimacy in experience approached or observed with piety in
order to accept what is there. All that is needed are the common
terms of our tradition together with some familiarity with the
habits of English verse and a responsiveness to a handful of
literary allusions which are, or used to be, universally permitted
and expected. I mean the allusions which are very nearly a part
of the substance of our mind, so early were they bred in us by
education and conversation: the allusions we can make without
consciousness of their meanings, but which, when we do become
conscious of their meanings, are like thunder and lightning and
the letting go of breath. A thing is what it is, and is its own
meaning, which might seem to us, as it did to Dante in his
Paradiso, a condition of blessedness, though in our context of
reading and writing we take tautology as the face of obfuscation
and irrelevance. Ripeness is all. A thing is what it is, and when
you can say so you will have made an allegory of direct statement—a statement so full of itself that it promises an ultimate
comprehensibility; it prefigures what is in its nature to be ful-
filled, either backwards or forwards, as is just.

Here is such an example of direct allegory, the last quatrain of
"The Good Man in Hell":

> One doubt of evil would bring down such a grace,
>   Open such a gate, all Eden could enter in,
> Hell be a place like any other place,
>   And love and hate and life and death begin.

This looks backwards, through a little theology, into our most backward selves where we abort, but need not, human action in the hell of the willfully wrong affirmation: it is that lethargy of sensation, or boredom of perception, which feels only the wrong good. Here is another allegory, which though it returns to Homer, had better be said to look forward. The poem is called "The Return," and it may be that the final phase of our pilgrimage, whatever earlier routes it took, is always a return, at least it would seem so to those of us in middle age or beyond. To the Ulysses who wanes in each of us in long hankering there is Penelope waxing ahead: the *gnostos*, the home-coming, the return, which constitutes by magic certainty, like the octave in music, the farthest reach of the journey.

> The doors flapped open in Ulysses' house,
> The lolling latches gave to every hand,
> Let traitor, babbler, tout and bargainer in.
> The rooms and passages resounded
> With ease and chaos of a public market,
> The walls mere walls to lean on as you talked,
> Spat on the floor, surveyed some newcomer
> With an absent eye. There you could be yourself.
> Dust in the nooks, weeds nodding in the yard,
> The thick walls crumbling. Even the cattle came
> About the doors with mild familiar stare
> As if this were their place.
> All around the island stretched the clean blue sea.
>
> Sole at the house's heart Penelope
> Sat at her chosen task, endless undoing
> Of endless doing, endless weaving, unweaving,
> In the clean chamber. Still her loom ran empty
> Day after day. She thought: "Here I do nothing
> Or less than nothing, making an emptiness
> Amid disorder, weaving, unweaving the lie

The day demands. Ulysses, this is duty,
To do and undo, to keep a vacant gate
Where order and right and hope and peace can enter.
Oh will you ever return? Or are you dead,
And this wrought emptiness my ultimate emptiness? "

She wove and unwove and wove and did not know
That even then Ulysses on the long
And winding road of the world was on his way.

This poem needs no commentary by way of discussion, for it invites the comment of attachment, of intimacy. It is a plaque of incarnation affixed to the wall of the mind, where, looking, you could be yourself. There is no end to the journey that is at hand. Let us say that this is a poem of great tenderness, the tenderness of human action which stretches between one being and another and stretches most in absence, most of all in the absence in the same room, and yet is the tenderness, which is the life, of actual possibility, confirming it even in the snapping point of failure. In our beginnings are our ends, all a return. To repeat, if the good man in hell broke lethargy, Penelope creates the live waiting which is also attention commanded. Each is annunciation bringing incarnation.

If so the poems themselves are epiphanies, like those green ones Stephen Dedalus meant to write, for epiphany—the showing of what is already made—is as far as the mind can go with what is wanted or needed. The verse makes only the analogous incarnation of the thing—its mere behavior—into words and forms that sometimes become poetry. But the secondary often leads us back to the primary, to what is still first; so let us look a little at the kind of poet Muir is, at his equipment in verse, and at the ideas and habits of mind that beset him in his epiphany of his grand theme.

As to the kind of poetry which Muir writes, it is the kind we all live in our salutations, our aversions, and our reveries—when we cry out, turn aside, or let the dreams within us work themselves into shape beyond our normal shaping powers. He is like all of us in those moments when we put meaning into our words. Only he is better than most of us are, for the shapes and meanings last for others' use: they become common currency in motion. There are no monuments here, either of imagination or ambition, and no bids for power and domination. There are, rather, gestures of recognition and intimations of the forms of all these. We are in their presence, as Shakespeare says water is in water, or as Burns says the snowflakes are on the black river. Only it is not Shakespeare and not Burns. This is what is meant by saying that Muir is not a professional poet, not even a public poet. Neither the open nor the overweening career was ever his. This is not Milton, who knew and overpassed his powers, but Milton's secretary, the Member from Hull, Andrew Marvell, who pursued his best possibilities and was several times seized by powers beyond himself—the same powers that sometimes seize us. Or let us say that Muir is like Traherne, who rehearsed traditional mysteries, rather than like Donne, for whom none of the traditions and no mere rehearsal was ever enough. Perhaps Muir is like George Herbert without a parish or a doctrine or any one temple to construct. He made secular what was his own, which was indeed how he saw it even when it was supernatural in its mode of contact, in annunciation and resurrection. His poems and no doubt his life were topical only to himself, and we make him our topic in the common place between us. He made a commonplace book in our own language.

Such is Muir's kind of poetry, and there ought to be a name for the kind. No doubt Mr. Northrop Frye will provide us with a good one (for he knows how we take hold of things better by a name than by the substance), but in the meantime we can say that it springs from an old and natural tradition like sunlight or breathing and is about as hard to do without, until we take our summers on the moon. I think there would be neither great poetry nor amusing poetry nor the grand folly of private poetry if there were not also—aware of all these—the steady poetry of the kind written by Muir. This poetry is a kind of thinking in verse, which is a very different thing from versifying thought, for the verse is the vital mode rather than the mere mode of the thought and is thus the substance of what we remember as well as the memorable form. It is a thinking in verse—as thinking in algebra or in farming or in love—which so far as it reaches form is poetry alive with the action of the mind, and which when it does not reach form has the dullness of the active mind failing. Almost none of our brains, as Darwin knew, are good for very much thinking, in verse or otherwise. Thoughts that fail in poetry are like dogs that have lost the scent.

Some brook has run between or a swamp sogs under the feet, and the life runs out of the flurry of action. Where the hound gives up and denies his interest the poet goes on willy-nilly, more dogged than any dog, so long as there is any verse to help him pretend a course or a spoor. Somewhere, across some gap or dark occasion, what is lost may be recovered. I take it Muir means something like this in another language—which has the desperateness of the certainty of what approaches saying and cannot be said—when he ends his autobiography in the following way:

> In the infinite web of things and events chance must be something different from what we think it to be. To comprehend that is not given to us, and to think of it is to recognize a

mystery, and to acknowledge the necessity of faith. As I look back on the part of the mystery which is my own life, my own fable, what I am most aware of is that we receive more than we can ever give; we receive it from the past, on which we draw with every breath, but also—and this is a point of faith—from the Source of the mystery itself, by the means which religious people call Grace.

Muir was looking back at the perennial mystery, and perhaps the perennial philosophy, of his whole life; I am looking at the mystery of the practice of writing verse. There is some place where the views cross.

One such place perhaps may be seen in the type of verse which Muir characteristically writes when the verse comes nearest to thought—when the words contribute to and indeed almost occasion the thought. The words precipitate, they do not distill the thought. Muir makes no epigrams in the modern sense in words which in themselves flash the wit; as a poet he is singularly little in love with words, and his words never make us blush. He makes no apothegms nor gnostic sayings either; there is no special penetration and no special mystery of knowledge; he observes by habit, rather, that way of words which goes with ritual and makes runes: he makes an old script, an older and different alphabet, out of the general mystery and the common institution, inescapably present, when looked at, in our regular vocabulary of word and myth and attitude. He has the great advantage of the power to re-create or transform them. His own poems make the best commentary on the distinction I want to set forth. Here is the end of "Ballad of Hector in Hades":

> Two shadows racing on the grass,
>   Silent and so near,
> Until his shadow falls on mine.
>   And I am rid of fear.

> The race is ended. Far away
> I hang and do not care,
> While round bright Troy Achilles whirls
> A corpse with streaming hair.

One does not even need to have read the *Iliad*, unless as a child; everything to do with Troy is part of our natural possession—a gift of our past—and all our languages have so constantly, if irregularly, repossessed themselves of it that every fresh statement of it, every variation or addition, has a natural authenticity. Hector and Achilles might well have been taken up by Freud along with Oedipus and Narcissus, for at least within our psyches we all run in great heat around that wall, and it makes little difference whether the other fellow is Hector or Achilles. In the eschatology of the psyche, Hades is not so judgmatical as the Christian hell, and our roles continue to reverse themselves, nightmare to nightmare, as they do in ordinary life. Our nightmares are the playmasters of our minds, and none are so masterly as our Greek nightmares. Homer has them all in their urgent and obliterative forms; Ovid their urbane forms; Muir, when he tackles them in his verse, their therapeutic and reminding forms.

Surely there is no cliché of nightmare so universal, touching so sharply upon us all, as the corpse with streaming hair; Achilles (and it could have been Hector) in this poem is only a *figura* for the figures with whom we are in perpetual pursuit in our private Hades. It is our nightmares which wake us as we have lost our next-to-last breath, and with what is left we make a rune or die, and there is a wide emptiness all around us, in which our senses and our decisions swim in common vertigo, accusing and self-accusing. This is the rune for the corpse with the streaming hair; and I will only remind you that the Duke of Clarence, just before he was visited by his murderers, saw in that dream of

his which "lengthened after life" (*Richard the Third*, I, iv)
"A shadow like an angel, with bright hair / Dabbled in blood."
Clarence, like Hector, spoke from the private Hades of the
psyche, and he, too, made a rune.

From "The Enchanted Knight" I quote the first and the last
two stanzas.

> Lulled by La Belle Dame Sans Merci he lies
> In the bare wood below the blackening hill.
> The plough drives nearer now, the shadow flies.
> Past him across the plain, but he lies still.
>
> . . . . .
>
> When a bird cries within the silent grove
> The long-lost voice goes by, he makes to rise
> And follow, but his cold limbs never move,
> And on the turf unstirred his shadow lies.
>
> But if a withered leaf should drift
> Across his face and rest, the dread drops start
> Chill on his forehead. Now he tries to lift
> The insulting weight that stays and breaks his heart.

No one needs to know Keats's poem, any more than Keats
needed to know the literary and folk sources for the belief in
the fatal destructiveness of love in one of its roles upon which his
poem—and Muir's—depends. The belief had a cave home in
some furthest source within us—perhaps in some anterior metamorphosis of the psyche in which love and its inspirations
exacted their cost more vividly than now and charged daring
more quickly with its natural end. As we think in an earlier
form of ourselves, so we use a different alphabet of feelings; and
in that form and that alphabet we believe preciously in what
in its present form we greet only with the attraction of horror.
The verse restores the early form by giving its thought a mode

of action. All Muir's poem except one word is a rune and ritual celebration of that dread lady—Robert Graves's White Goddess—who takes back in one moment not only her gift to her lover but also his life itself; the one word is the word "insulting," a modern and moody word, by which the poet expresses his rebellion against the tradition and his denial of the ritual, the while it breaks him down. It is as if Muir thought for a moment like Dostoevsky, where the last gasp of the individual is in insult and injury and laceration. The history of the word "insult" is present here whether Muir knew it or not: as a frequentative form of the verb *insilare*, to leap upon. The rain of insult is perpetual while life lasts. This poem, then, is a rune in old ballad form, to express and purge the nightmare of the White Goddess.

The poem called "The Island" goes beyond the condition of rune and makes a spell out of the glamour or secret art of grammar. The island of the title is not Muir's birthplace, the island of Orkney, but Sicily, the visible merging place for all our histories, teeming as it does with living people, with the races and beliefs and arts of other times, especially teeming with beliefs, some now quite lost to conscious memory. In Sicily erosion and fertility compete in every mode: "Harvests of men to give men birth." All this is only less so for the island of Orkney, for we survive, as it were, only in islands. Here is the end of the poem.

> And self-begotten cycles close
> About our way; indigenous art
> And simple spells make unafraid
> The haunted labyrinths of the heart,
> And with our wild succession braid
> The resurrection of the rose.

Possibly it should be emphasized that it is the indigenous art and the simple spells that make the braid. Indigenous art is innate form. To make the indigenous simple is to make the spell of rational imagination with which both to purge and to involve our wild succession.

That is to say, in the work of a man like Muir whose mind has no temptation either to remake the world or to reason it out of existence, the rational imagination here makes its maximum task to recapture tradition in direct apprehension, to find in what happens to him an Illumination in the linkage of the chances that have gone before with the abstractions that persist. It is as if, with Muir, allegory were the indigenous and final art. As he says,

> Or so I dream when at my door
> I hear my soul, my visitor.

And when he says this he reminds us of Emily Dickinson and how we might reassess her along the same lines, but with a different and perhaps larger stretch, as those that contain Muir. Muir is a Dickinson with a different deficiency. But both poets resorted naturally to all the tradition to which they were exposed, and they made their resort to find abstractions in which their problematic—even their unseemly—sensibilities could be united with their selves. Muir's resort was to the Greek and classical, to the Christian, and to the monstrous forms or postures of the psyche that precede all our taxonomy, and it is these forms that he set about putting to the commonest musics he could find: the sonnet, the ballad, the anecdote, and the commonest diction he could hear—not the language of the street, but the general language of literature. The two provided means for the discernment of the memorable, since it was in the service of memory that both had grown up. Here one thinks of Valéry's remark,

that one keeps in memory only what one has not understood, or
of that poet's other remark that Reason (and this is her warrant
of office) admires the monuments (the cities of imagination)
that she could not herself have built. In Muir it is sometimes
the actual damaged monuments of true cities only in our lifetime
truncated from their stories, like the city of Prague, which he
loved, and which is the subject of the poem, "The Good Town."
Plato, Augustine, Dante and (in a small, persistent pang)
Baudelaire did this, and so Muir. Cities are like annunciations,
visits of the soul on our grandest human scale in monumental
analogy to the everlasting devastations of the moment seized.

> Whether the soul at first
> This pilgrimage began,
> Or the shy body leading
> Conducted soul to soul
> Who knows? This is the most
> That soul and body can,
> To make us each for each
> And in our spirit whole.

These lines, which end a poem called "The Annunciation,"
make a wooing of that goddess, other than the White Goddess
who makes us die, who makes us live, the personal city within
the great. There is a poem called simply "Song"—the simple
spell of indigenous art—where the two cities are in piety joined.
It is the song of the thought Muir put most in his verse.

> The quarrel from the start,
> Long past and never past,
> The war of mind and heart,
> The great war and the small
> That tumbles the hovel down
> And topples town on town
> Come to one place at last:
> Love gathers all.

One observes here that Muir's most direct statement reaches to the purest abstraction. He is like this even when his concern is in the immediate mood of the crash of melancholy and joy. I would cite, for they are too much to repeat here in full, the ends of the twin poems called "Dejection" and "Sorrow."

> For every eloquent voice dies in this air
> Wafted from anywhere to anywhere
> And never counted by the careful clock,
> That cannot strike the hour
> Of power that will dissolve this power
> Until the rock rise up and split the rock.
>
> ———
>
> If it were only so . . .
> But right and left I find
> Sorrow, sorrow,
> And cannot be resigned,
> Knowing that we were made
> By joy to drive joy's trade
> And not to waver to and fro,
> But quickly go.

It was just said that these things are in piety joined, and piety is not an artichoke to be pulled apart for the eating, with the most part discarded. We have here, in the language of Croce about Virgil, which we began by quoting, "a human feeling of bitter memories, of shuddering horror, of melancholy, of home-sickness, of tenderness, of a kind of childish pietás"; and we must not tamper with it like psychiatrists, but become intimate with it without assault, like fellow-humans. It is with piety that we recognize our familiars, even when they are horrors or our inmost selves, but most when we see we should be nothing at all without them. It is with piety that we make the best order out of our stories. If we need an abstraction or a generalization to grasp and share what Muir's thinking in verse is up to, it is in our best conception of the piety of the story. For there is a piety in Muir—and like humility, in a hair's breadth it will be pride or humiliation—towards nature, the cross, the Greeks, death, time, love, old age, and to the obsessions of all these and their nightmares. For our nightmares only smother us where we have paid too much attention to our real life.

Now to repeat, since even a story must repeat itself to be true, wherever Mr. Muir himself is, the inner motion of his poetry still draws from the "carnival of birth and death," as he calls it, of the Orkney sea-farm where he grew up. Muir is an island man and is full of natural piety—a phrase Wordsworth put into poetry. But where Wordsworth observed it, and sought it, Muir's poems exert his natural piety, as a function of his being; exert it equally to the hill and the plough, to the stars and to his Visitor, the Soul, never forgetting the one when he greets the other. His poetry participates without prejudice in the warfare between the two elements of the tradition which moves him. I do not think this warfare very different from the war of the journey and the war of the pity which inhabited the mind of Dante, and I think it is in this sense that Muir is a traditional poet; he deals with the wars of our journey and our pity. His order—whether in his prosody of ballad and sonnet and blank verse or in his themes of the human condition—is as old as the terms of experience and the reach of thought; but everywhere there is the wildness of fresh disorder which is the current of life in his order. If the wildness is reminiscent of eternity both before and after, so much the better. The regular is most wild.

All this is vivid in the poems themselves. Here is the other of the two poems he has called "The Return." (The first was that with which we began, regarding Penelope awaiting Ulysses.)

> . . . And the voices,
> Sweeter than any sound dreamt of or known,
> Call me, recall me. I draw near at last,
> An old old man, and scan the ancient walls
> Rounded and softened by the compassionate years,
> The old and heavy and long-leaved trees that watch
> This my inheritance in friendly darkness.
> And yet I cannot enter, for all within
> Rises before me there, rises against me,
> A sweet and terrible labyrinth of longing,
> So that I turn aside and take the road
> That always, early or late, runs on before.

And here are the last distichs of "Epitaph" and "Comfort in Self-Despite."

> If now is Resurrection, then let stay
> Only what's ours when this is put away.

———

> So I may yet recover by this bad
> Research that good I scarcely dreamt I had.

In Mr. J. C. Hall's introduction to the *Collected Poems*, Stephen Spender is quoted as saying that Muir witnessed everywhere in Rome the climactic symbol of Resurrection. To this Mr. Hall adds a footnote. "Edwin Muir tells me that the symbol which impressed him in Rome was that of Incarnation, not Resurrection." To me, both seem right, and the two fragments of verse which I have just read attest it. In Muir's poems both Resurrection and Incarnation—the rediscovery and the bodying forth—are going on at the same time. That is why so much of the poetry is nearly not words at all, but the action of the mind itself taking thought of Resurrection and Incarnation, the carnival of birth and death. Like Prospero, that great persona of human piety, this poet would still his beating mind.

This love a moment known
For what I do not know
And in a moment gone
Is like the happy doe
That keeps its perfect laws
Between the tiger's paws
And vindicates its cause.

Between the tiger's paws Muir stills his beating mind.

Yvor Winters

Poetic

Styles,

Old and New

THE SHORT POEM OF THE LATE middle ages, of the sixteenth century, and of the early seventeenth century was usually rational in structure, and in fact was very often logical. This structure began to break down toward the middle of the seventeenth century: the signs are most obvious in *Lycidas*, but one can find them in Marvell and Vaughan and elsewhere. The rational structure was often used for unreasonable ends, as in much of Sidney and Donne, but the structure is almost always there. These facts are well known to scholars by now, and they may seem unworthy of mention; but they appear to be unknown to many of our critics, and I need to call attention to them for the sake of what I shall say later. Within this rational frame, however, there were two main schools of poetry in the sixteenth century and earlier: on the one hand there were the poets of the plain style, and on the other hand the poets of the style which has been variously labeled courtly, ornate, sugared, or Petrarchan. Some poets employed both methods, but most poets worked mainly in one or

the other, for the difference was a difference of principle, and
the principles were commonly understood. Wyatt, Gascoigne,
Raleigh, Greville, and Jonson wrote mainly in the plain style.
Sidney and Spenser can serve as examples of the courtly.

Donne can hardly be described as courtly or sugared, but he is
ornate, and to this extent Petrarchan. Donne is only super-
ficially a rebel against the tradition of Sidney; essentially he is a
continuator, at least in a large number of his poems. His mind
is more complex than that of Sidney, and more profound; his
temperament is more violent and more perverse; his virtues and
his vices are more striking; but in most of his famous poems he
is working in the same tradition. At this time I can refer to
only one of his poems: the *Valediction Forbidding Mourning*.

The poem is so well known that I need not quote it. The
entire poem, like most of Donne's poems, is hyperbolic: he over-
states his case violently, in a manner which, in our time, is called
dramatic. The theme of the poem, though fairly serious, is also
simple: that is, the lovers are united by their rational souls
rather than by their sensible souls, and their love is therefore
relatively stable, and they can endure a physical parting more
easily than can those lovers who are united merely by sense.
This idea in itself is an overstatement, and Donne, of all people,
must have been aware of the fact: this overstatement is part of
the hyperbole. But there is more than this in the hyperbole:
there are the metaphors and similes. The figures in the first
twelve lines are both trite and ridiculous. Mr. Cleanth Brooks
says that some of the same figures in *The Canonization* are
offered as parody; I doubt this, but they are not offered as parody
here. They are offered here in absolute seriousness, and they are
bad. But this is not the main point, as far as I am concerned at
present. The main point is that they are ornament, decoration.

They say very little about the subject, say it loosely, and say it with a kind of naïve violence. Jonson could have said more in two lines than Donne says in twelve.

The decoration in the opening lines is bad decoration, but later the decoration is good. The gold and the compasses are brilliant and they have made the poem famous; nevertheless, the gold and the compasses are decoration. The gold and the compasses tell us nothing about the lovers, really, except that they are inseparable in terms of the rational soul, yet the gold and the compasses are sensory details. There is much reference to sensory—usually visual—detail in Renaissance poetry which is not meant to be visualized; I shall have more to say of this later. But the gold and the compasses are meant to be visualized, or if they are not so meant, Donne out-did himself. Yet we do not visualize the lovers either as gold or as compasses: if we did so, the poem would become preposterous. We visualize the gold and the compasses and between these and the lovers there is a very general, an almost uncertain, intellectual correspondence. It is the gold and the compasses which save these passages, and very nearly in their own right. The passages are ornament, or very nearly so. They are very quotable, and have often been quoted. They are quotable because they are detachable; they are detachable because they are attached.

It is foolish to say, with Mr. Eliot, that Donne thinks with his sense (that is, his sensible soul); he thinks with his rational soul, and he often ornaments his thought with his sensory perception, sometimes well and sometimes badly. The formula is Horatian: profit and pleasure—profit from reason, pleasure from sensory perception or other decoration. The formula is common in the Renaissance, but it is not the only formula possible in the Renaissance or at other times. The formula of our own time which corresponds in part to the Horatian formula is that of tenor and vehicle, although the modern formula has a wider applicability. In Donne's poem the constancy of the lovers is the tenor; the gold and the compasses are vehicles; the vehicles are more interesting than the tenor; therefore they are ornament, and the tenor—the essential theme—suffers. In our time the most famous Renaissance vehicle, as far as I know, has been Marvell's chariot. It functions in much the same way as Donne's gold and compasses.

In Shakespeare's sonnets we find both plain and ornate styles, sometimes in the same poem, but both, more often than not, in a state of decay; and we find also the only decay of rational structure which I can recollect among the major poets of the time. I intend now to discuss some of Shakespeare's sonnets, and next two of Jonson's major poems, and then to draw a few conclusions.

II

There are few of Shakespeare's sonnets which do not show traces of genius, and genius of an unusually beguiling kind; and in a fair number we have more than traces. Yet in the past ten years or so I have found them more and more disappointing.[1]

In the first place there is in a large number of the poems an attitude of servile weakness on the part of the poet in the face of the person addressed; this attitude is commonly so marked

---

[1] John Crowe Ransom antedates me by quite a few years in this heresy. See his essay "Shakespeare at Sonnets" in *The World's Body* (1938). Ransom's objections and my own are similar in some respects and different in others. My own tardiness in seeing Shakespeare's weaknesses is evidence (a) of the effect of established habit on critical judgment and (b) of the curious way in which a shifting mixture of the good and the bad can produce a result which it is difficult to judge objectively.

as to render a sympathetic approach to the subject all but impossible, in spite of any fragmentary brilliance which may be exhibited. It will not do to reply that this is a convention of the courtly style and should not be taken seriously. If it is a convention of the courtly style, then it is a weakness in that style. But it is not an invariable quality of the courtly poets; it occurs very seldom in poets of the plain style; and Shakespeare seems to mean it seriously.

In the second place, Shakespeare seldom takes the sonnet form with any real seriousness. The sonnets are almost invariably conceived in very simple terms and are developed through simple repetition or antithesis, so that they never achieve the closely organized treatment of the subject which we find in the best of Jonson and Donne. This weakness is often aggravated by the fact that Shakespeare frequently poses his problem and then solves it by an evasion or an irrelevant cliché: this is more or less the method of the courtly style at its weakest, but the element of genius which goes into many of these sonnets raises one's expectations to the point that one cannot take this sort of triviality with good grace.

In the third place, Shakespeare often allows his sensitivity to the connotative power of language to blind him to the necessity for sharp denotation, with the result that a line or passage or even a whole poem may disappear behind a veil of uncertainty: in this last weakness he is even farther from his major contemporaries than in any of the others. I shall endeavor to illustrate these weaknesses as they occur in poems which I shall discuss.

I will begin with LXVI:

> Tir'd with all these, for restful death I cry
> As to behold desert a beggar born,

And needy nothing trimm'd in jollity,
And purest faith unhappily forsworn,
And gilded honor shamefully misplac'd,
And maiden virtue rudely strumpeted,
And right perfection wrongfully disgrac'd,
And strength by limping sway disabled,
And art made tongue-tied by authority,
And folly—doctor-like—controlling skill,
And simple truth miscalled simplicity,
And captive good attending captain ill:
    Tir'd with all these, from these I would be gone,
    Save that, to die, I leave my love alone.

This is one of a number of Elizabethan poems dealing with dis-illusionment with the world. Others are Gascoigne's "Wood-manship," "The Lie" by Raleigh, and "False world, goodnight," by Ben Jonson. But whereas Gascoigne, Raleigh, and Jonson offer the best solutions that they can, Raleigh with righteous defiance, Gascoigne and Jonson with a combination of scorn for corruption and Christian acceptance of the individual fate, Shakespeare (like Arnold after him, in "Dover Beach") turns aside from the issues he has raised to a kind of despairing senti-mentality, and the effect is one of weakness, poetic and per-sonal. The same thing occurs in many other sonnets: for examples XXIX ("When in disgrace with fortune and men's eyes") and XXX ("When to the sessions of sweet silent thought"). I do not wish to deny the many felicities in these poems, for they are real; but the poems do not rise to the occa-sions which they invoke. The poem which I have just quoted would be a fine example of the plain style, except for the couplet, which represents sentimental degeneration of the courtly rhetoric.

It would be easy to make a list of inept phrases from the sonnets. The clichés, for example, are numerous and well known, and so are the bad plays on words ("When first your eye I eyed"). But most poets sin in this fashion much of the time, or in some comparable fashion. There is another kind of weak phrasing in Shakespeare, however, which is prevalent in his work and more serious than the cliché or the bad pun; it is characteristic of later ages rather than his own, and it sets him apart from his great contemporaries. This is his use of words for some vague connotative value, with little regard for exact denotation. An interesting example occurs in CXVI:

> Let me not to the marriage of true minds
> Admit impediments. Love is not love
> Which alters when it alteration finds,
> Or bends with the remover to remove:
> O no! it is an ever-fixed mark,
> That looks on tempests and is never shaken;
> It is the star to every wandering bark,
> Whose worth's unknown, although his height be taken.
> Love's not Time's fool, though rosy lips and cheeks
> Within his bending sickle's compass come;
> Love alters not with his brief hours and weeks,
> But bears it out even to the edge of doom.
>   If this be error and upon me proved,
>   I never writ, nor no man ever loved.

The difficulty here resides in the word *worth*. The fixed star, which guides the mariner, is compared to true love, which guides the lover. The mariner, by taking the height of the star, can estimate his position at sea, despite the fact that he knows nothing of the star's "worth." *Worth*, with reference to the star, probably means astrological influence, though it might mean something else. The lover, by fixing his mind on the concept of true love, similarly can guide himself in his personal life. But what does *worth*, as distinct from height, mean in this second connection? For the lover can scarcely guide himself by a concept of true love, he can scarcely indeed have a concept of true love, unless he has some idea of the worth of true love. The comparison blurs at this point, and with it the meaning. One may perhaps push the astrological influence here and say that the lover, although he has a general knowledge of the nature and virtue (if virtue can be separated from worth) of true love, yet does not know precisely the effect upon him that true love will have. But this will not do: he obviously knows something of the effect, for the rest of the poem says that he does. There is simply no such separation between the two functions of true love as there is between the two functions of the star, yet the comparison is made in such a way as to indicate a separation.

This kind of thing does not occur in Greville or Donne or Jonson. Even in the more ornate Sidney—for example in the clumsy figurative language of " Leave me, O love "—it is usually possible to follow the thought even though the figure may be mishandled. But here one loses the thought. Greville, in " Down in the depth," employs the language of theology; Donne employs the language of astrology (and other technical language) in the " Valediction of my Name in a Window." Nothing is lost by this precision, but on the contrary there is a gain, for the emotion cannot have force when its nature and origin are obscure. Shakespeare contents himself here with a vague feeling of the mysterious and the supernatural, and the feeling is very vague indeed.

The sonnet is characteristic in other respects. The successive quatrains do not really develop the theme; each restates it. This makes, perhaps, for easy absorption on the part of the more or less quiescent reader, but it makes also for a somewhat simple and uninteresting poetry. The sonnet form is short, and the

90952

great poet should endeavor to use it more efficiently, to say as much as can be said of his subject within its limits; such efficiency is never characteristic of Shakespeare. Lines nine and ten are clichés, which are barely rescued by an habitual grace, and the concluding couplet is a mere tag, which has no dignity or purpose in relationship to the sonnet or within itself. Yet the first four lines have precision, dignity, and simplicity, which are moving, and the twelfth line has subdued grandeur, due in part to the heavy inversion of the third foot and to the heavy anapest and iamb following. The high reputation of the sonnet is due about equally, I suspect, to its virtues and its faults.

One of the most perplexing of the sonnets is CVII:

> Not mine own fears, nor the prophetic soul
> Of the wide world, dreaming on things to come,
> Can yet the lease of my true love control,
> Supposed as forfeit to a confin'd doom.
> The mortal moon hath her eclipse endured,
> And the sad augurs mock their own presage;
> Incertitudes now crown themselves assured,
> And peace proclaims olives of endless age.
> Now with the drops of this most balmy time
> My love looks fresh, and death to me subscribes,
> Since, spite of him, I'll live in this poor rime,
> While he insults o'er dull and speechless tribes:
>   And thou in this shalt find thy monument
>   When tyrants' crests and tombs of brass are spent.

The sonnet has given rise to a great deal of scholarly speculation, most of which the reader can find summarized in Rollins's variorum edition of the sonnets. One of the commonest interpretations is that which identifies the mortal moon with Elizabeth and the eclipse with her death. The friend, then, is Southampton, who was released from prison upon the accession of James, and lines six, seven, eight, nine, and ten refer to the general fears that there would be civil disorder upon the death of Elizabeth and to the fact that James was nevertheless crowned with no disorder. The interpretation is fairly plausible, though by no means certain; but it involves two difficulties which, I think, have never been met. The tone of the poem is scarcely explained by this interpretation: the tone is sombre and mysterious, as if supernatural forces were under consideration—this tone is most obvious in the first quatrain, but it persists throughout. Furthermore, in line eleven we have a monstrous non sequitur, for there is not the remotest connection between Southampton's release from prison or the events leading up to it and Shakespeare's making himself and Southampton immortal in verse. To this objection the reader may reply that the concluding lines are merely in a Petrarchan convention and should not be taken too seriously. They may represent such a convention, but they have to be taken seriously, for the tone of seriousness and mystery, the magnificence of the language, are such that we are not prepared for triviality at this point. If this interpretation (or I think any other in the variorum editions) is accepted, then the poem stands as one of the most striking examples of Shakespeare's inability to control his language, of his tendency to indulge vague emotion with no respect for meaning. And the poem may, in fact, be such an example.

Leslie Hotson, however, has come forward with another theory.[2] He believes that the mortal moon (mortal: deadly, death-dealing) is the Spanish Armada, of which the line of battle was moon shaped, and which attacked England and was defeated in 1588, a year of which there had been dire predictions for

[2] *Shakespeare's Sonnets Dated, and other essays*, by Leslie Hotson (London, 1949).

generations, some of the prophets having thought it the year in which the world would end. Hotson is an irritating writer, as everyone who has read him carefully must know. But whatever objections one may have to Hotson's theory, there is no denying the fact that he documents it fully and impressively. Furthermore—and this is a point which Hotson fails to mention—this interpretation explains the mysterious tone of the poem (for in these terms we are dealing literally with supernatural forces, as well as with the most terrifying of natural forces), and it eliminates the non sequitur (for the lives of both the poet and the friend had been threatened, and both have survived). Hotson's theory clarifies the poem at every point, in spite of the conventional elements in the poem and the obscurely allusive manner of writing.

One can make certain obvious objections to Hotson's theory. For example, Hotson claims that the entire sequence was done by the age of twenty-five: this in spite of the facts that Shakespeare repeatedly refers to himself as an aging man and that there are many parallels in phrasing between the sonnets and the later plays. Furthermore, Hotson bases this claim on the explication of only one sonnet other than the sonnet just discussed. The management of the iambic pentameter line would seem to be too sensitive and skillful for a young man in 1588, although anything, of course, is possible when we are dealing with a poet of genius. But in favor of Hotson's view would be the very weaknesses which I have been describing—weaknesses which might well be those of a young man—although Hotson appears to be unaware of them. However, these weaknesses might easily be those of an older man, more at home in the dramatic form, writing carelessly for a private audience, and working in a style which in the course of his mature life became obsolete. Even with Hotson's explanation, however, or with another as good, the poem is faulty. No poem is wholly self-contained, but most poems work within frames of reference which are widely understood. This poem appears to have a very particular frame of reference about which it will always be impossible to be sure. The poem is almost all connotation, with almost no denotation; it is almost purely vehicle, with almost no tenor; it is almost wholly ornament, with almost nothing to which the ornament can be attached. It would be easy to say that such a poem is a kind of forerunner of some of the deliberately obscure work of the past hundred years; but this work is all based on closely related theories—those of Mallarmé or of Pound, for examples—and Shakespeare had no such theories. Shakespeare's ideas about the nature of poetry were those of his age, but he was often unable to write in accordance with them. Such a poem as this must have been the result of inadvertence.

Whatever the faults of the sonnets as wholes, their incidental beauties are numerous. These beauties are often of the most elusive kind, and they are probably felt by many readers without ever being identified. Consider, for example, line six of Sonnet XIX:

> And do Whate'er thou wilt, swift-footed Time.

There is a plaintive desperation in the line which it is impossible to describe but which any sensitive reader can feel. In what is being said there is a stereotyped but real and timeless fear, and this is expressed in part by the helplessness of the imperative and in part by the archaic cliché *swift-footed*. It is expressed also in the emphases of the rhythmical pattern: the first three feet are all heavily accented, but each succeeding foot more heavily than the one preceding, so that we reach a climax on *wilt*, followed by the long pause of the comma, the pause in turn followed by a foot lighter and more evenly stressed, and this by a very heavily stressed foot. This is not an original line nor a great one; it is derivative and minor—but it is moving.

More obvious are the moral perceptions in the second quatrain of XXIX:

> When in disgrace with fortune and men's eyes
> I all alone beweep my outcast state,
> And trouble deaf heaven with my bootless cries,
> And look upon myself, and curse my fate,
> Wishing me like to one more rich in hope,
> Featur'd like him, like him with friends possessed,
> Desiring this man's art, and that man's scope,
> With what I most enjoy contented least;
> Yet in these thoughts myself almost despising,
> Haply I think on thee,—and then my state,
> Like to the lark at break of day arising
> From sullen earth, sings hymns at heaven's gate;
>> For thy sweet love remember'd such wealth brings
>> That then I scorn to change my state with kings.

The first quatrain of this sonnet is a passable example of what the French would call *la poésie larmoyante*; it is facile melancholy at its worst. And yet the next four lines are precise and admirable; they are a fine example of the plain style. In the third quatrain we have the lark which has made the sonnet famous. The lark is an ornament, in the same way as Donne's compasses. In the last six lines we are told, of course, that the poet's state of mind has changed; and we are told why—he has thought of the friend or lady, whichever it may be. But this a sentimental, an almost automatic, change, and it is hard to understand after the four lines preceding. It is what I have previously called an evasion of the issue posed. And the lark is a sentimental lark: at the descriptive level, *sullen, sings hymns*, and *heaven's gate* are all inaccurate. The lark is burdened with the unexplained emotions of the poet. But the lark is not representative of any explanatory idea. The lark suffers in these ways from comparison with the pigeons of Wallace Stevens, of which I shall write briefly at the end of this essay. We have more lark than understanding in these lines, and more easy sentiment than lark.

One of the most fascinating passages is the description of the imperceptible but continuous action of Time in CIV:

> Ah! yet doth beauty like a dial hand
> Steal from his figure, and no pace perceived;
> So your sweet hue, which methinks still doth stand,
> Hath motion, and mine eye may be deceived.

And yet even here we are in grammatical difficulty, for it is the dial hand (or its shadow) which should steal from the figure; it is not beauty. Or if we take *figure* to mean the human form or face, then the dial hand is left with no reference, and there is no basis for the second half of the comparison. We understand the passage, of course, but the statement is careless.

One can find good poems among the sonnets which do not achieve at any point the greatness of certain lines from sonnets which fail. Such, for examples, are XXIII, CXXIX, and CXLVI. The first of these is correct but minor; the second ("The expense of spirit") is powerful in phrasing, but repetitious in structure—as Douglas Peterson has shown (*Shakespeare Quarterly* V-4), it derives its structure and much of its matter from a passage in Wilson's *Art of Rhetorique*—and appears to be a forceful exercise on a limited topic; the third is somewhat commonplace when compared with the best of Donne's *Holy Sonnets*.

The most impressive sonnet of all, I suspect, is LXXVII, in which the peculiarly Shakespearian qualities are put to good use, in which the peculiar faults are somehow transformed into virtues. Jonson, Donne, and Greville—indeed most of the great poets of the Renaissance—tend to deal with the experiential import of explicit definitions and sometimes to offer explicit and figurative excursions from definitions. In the plain style at its plainest, the passion with which the human significance of the definitions is felt is communicated by the emotional content of the language in which they are stated: that is, we do not have definition here and emotion there, but meaning and emotion coexist at every moment; in the relatively ornate style, the excursions are controlled in a general but clear way by the definitions. But Shakespeare's approach to his subject is indirect and evasive. In LXXVII the explicit subject is not very important: it provides the occasion for the entry into the poem of certain perceptions which appear to be almost accidental but which are really Shakespeare's obsessive themes.

LXXVII appears to have been written to accompany the gift of a blank book:

> Thy glass will show thee how thy beauties wear;
> Thy dial how thy precious minutes waste;
> The vacant leaves thy mind's imprint will bear,
> And of this book this learning may'st thou taste.
> The wrinkles which thy glass will truly show
> Of mouthed graves will give thee memory;
> Thou by thy dial's shady stealth may know
> Time's thievish progress to eternity.
> Look! what thy memory cannot contain
> Commit to these waste blanks, and thou shalt find
> Those children nursed, delivered from thy brain
> To take a new acquaintance of thy mind.

> These offices, so oft as thou wilt look,
> Shall profit thee and much enrich thy book.

The first quatrain states the ostensible theme of the poem: time passes and we age, yet by writing down our thoughts, we take a new acquaintance of our mind, acquire a new learning. The second quatrain enlarges upon the passage of time; the last six lines revert to the moralizing.

But something very strange occurs. The imperceptible coming of wrinkles displays the physical invasion of the enemy, just as the imperceptible movement of the dial's shadow displays the constant movement of the enemy. In the ninth line, however, the enemy invades the mind, the center of being; it was the figure of the book which enabled the poet to extend the poem to this brilliant and terrifying suggestion, yet so far as the development of the theme is concerned, the extension occurs almost by the way, as if it were a casual and merely incidental feeling.

> Look! What thy memory cannot contain
> Commit to these waste blanks . . . .

This command, in isolation, is merely a command to make good use of the book, and the remainder of the passage deals wholly with the advantages of doing so; yet the command follows the lines in which we have observed the destruction of the physical being by time, and in this position it suggests the destruction of the mind itself. This terrifying subject, the loss of identity before the uncontrollable invasion of the impersonal, is no sooner suggested than it is dropped.

There is a related but more curious employment of pure suggestion in the word *waste* in the same passage. The word is obviously a pun, with the emphasis on the secondary meaning.

It means not only *unused* or *blank* (this is the primary meaning, and it gives us a tautology), but it means *desert* or *uninhabited* or *uninhabitable*, a sense reinforced by the verb *waste* in the second line; but rationally considered, the pages are not waste in this second sense, but are instruments offered for actually checking the invasion of the waste. A feeling, in other words, is carried over from its proper motive to something irrelevant to it, and the dominant feeling is thus reinforced at the expense of the lesser; this dominant feeling, one should add, arises not from the ostensible theme of the poem—the book and its use—but from the incidental theme which has slipped into the poem. In order to express the invasion of confusion, the poem for a moment actually enters the realm of confusion instead of describing it. The poem, I think, succeeds; but after having examined the unsuccessful confusion of other sonnets, I cannot decide whether the success is due to skill or to accident.

III

The style of Ben Jonson is plain, but it is also urbane and polished. It has the solid structure of the styles of Gascoigne and Raleigh, with evidence of a knowledge of the flexibility of Sidney. Jonson is no such enraptured rhetorician as Sidney, but on the other hand his understanding of Sidneyan rhetoric prevents his indulging in any such affectation of roughness as we find to some extent in Gascoigne; he is freer from mannerism and a purer stylist than either, and, since he operates from a central position, he is more sensitive and more skillful than either, for he can employ the tones of both without committing himself wholly to one direction. Shakespeare, in comparison, succumbed to excessive and uncontrolled sensitivity; Donne shows the vices of both Gascoigne and Sidney, the affectation of harshness on the one hand and of sophisticated ingenuity on the other. Greville alone of this group rivals Jonson in control of his style and may surpass him in the range of his materials and the profundity of his thought; yet Jonson's style is more varied than Greville's and places him as the first master stylist of the plain tradition: that is to say, of the great tradition.

Jonson is a classicist in the best sense, and though his classicism is no doubt in part the result of his study of the Greek and Latin poets, critics, and rhetoricians, as it was probably in greater part the result of his natural bent, it is reasonable to see in his work a resolution of the qualities to be found in Sidney and the poets of the plain style. One does not learn to write English verse from studying Latin verse, though one may thus acquire applicable theories. Jonson must have been familiar with the poets whom I have mentioned; and these and a few others *were the English language*, so far as poetic style was concerned, at the time when Jonson was mastering the language, and there was little to distract the attention from them.

Like most of the lyrics of the period, Jonson's are expository in structure; but, unlike many, they engage in very little figurative excursion (such as one gets in Donne) and very little illustrative repetition (such as one gets in Nashe's " In Time of Pestilence "). They are very closely written arguments, or at least a good many of them are, and they have to be read very closely if one is not to lose the continuity of the arguments. He wrote a little devotional poetry of a high order, but his subject matter is chiefly ethical in the narrowest sense: that is, he deals with problems of conduct arising between one human being and another, or between one human being and the social group, or between one human being and other serious problems; indeed, his devotional poetry concerns itself explicitly with man's moral relationship with God. The language is accurate and concise with regard to both idea and feeling; there is an exact correlation between motive and feeling which may easily be mistaken for coldness and mechanical indifference by the reader accustomed to more florid enticements, but which impresses the present reader rather as integrity and nobility. Among Jonson's greatest poems illustrating these qualities are the following: "Though beauty be the mark of praise"; "Where dost thou careless lie"; "High-spirited friend"; "From death and dark oblivion near the same"; "False world, good night"; "Good and great God, can I not think of Thee"; "Let it not your wonder move"; and "To draw no envy, Shakespeare, on thy name."

I will begin with "An Elegy":

> Though beauty be the mark of praise,
>   And yours of whom I sing be such
>   As not the world can praise too much,
> Yet is't your virtue now I raise.
>
> A virtue like allay, so gone
>   Throughout your form, as though that move,
>   And draw and conquer all men's love,
> This subjects you to love of one.
>
> Wherein you triumph yet: because
>   'Tis of yourself, and that you use
>   The noblest freedom, not to choose
> Against or faith, or honor's laws.
>
> But who should less expect of you,
>   In whom alone love lives again?
>   By whom he is restored to men,
> And kept, and bred, and brought up true?
>
> His falling temples you have reared,
>   The withered garlands tane away;

His altars kept from the decay
That envy wished, and nature feared.

And on them burn so chaste a flame
    With so much loyalty's expense
    As love, t'acquit such excellence,
Is gone himself into your name.

And you are he: the Deity
    To whom all lovers are designed,
    That would their better objects find:
Among which faithful troup am I.

Who as an off'ring at your shrine,
    Have sung this hymn, and here entreat
    One spark of your diviner heat
To light upon a love of mine.

Which if it kindle not, but scant
    Appear, and that to shortest view,
    Yet give me leave t'adore in you
What I, in her, am grieved to want.

This is a poem in praise of a woman who is a friend, not the
beloved; she is praised for her virtue and her constancy in love,
at the expense of the woman whom the poet loves; and because
of these qualities she is identified with the god of love. The
theme is serious, and it is worked out in greater detail than my
summary would suggest. On the other hand, the theme is in no
wise difficult to understand, in spite of the compactness of the
writing.

The poem is far from simple, however, and much of it may
escape the reader who has read it for its paraphrasable content
alone. It is a fusion of two kinds of poetry: the song and the
didactic poem. It is a poem in praise of virtue in love; and, in
connection with love, the machinery of the old Religion of Love
(in which virtue as here conceived was scarcely an element) is

employed discreetly. The stanza frequently suggests a song stanza as it opens, and then seems to stop the song with a didactic close, as if strings had been plucked and then muted; and this effect, more or less inherent in the form of the stanza itself, is sometimes stressed and sometimes softened. In the first stanza, for example, the effect of the single-hearted love song is suggested in the first three lines, but qualified by *though* and by the harsh rimes *such* and *much*; and in the fourth line the tone is brought down firmly to the didactic. The second stanza suggests a song-movement throughout, and the subject of love in the second and third lines reinforces the movement; but the treatment of the subject is moralistic, and the song quality is softened by this fact. The third stanza is one of the most explicitly moralistic, yet the first clause suggests another tone, that of the triumphant love song; and this tone dominates the first three lines of the fourth stanza and is only partly muted in the fourth line. The fifth stanza resembles the fourth, but here the Religion of Love, which has been introduced quietly in the fourth, emerges strongly; and in the first two lines especially the accented syllables are heavy and long, and the unaccented are light, in such a way as to suggest a triumphal chant. In the remainder of the poem the didactic tone dominates, but it has already been so qualified by the other that the echo of the song is present most of the time, most plainly, perhaps, in the eighth stanza and most muted in the last.

It is all but impossible to describe the nuances of feeling which I have been trying to describe. The reader who comes to this poem must have a reasonably full acquaintance with the Elizabethan songs and with the tradition of the plain style; he must understand metrical structure and the various methods of rhythmic variation; and he must read carefully. There is nothing wasted in this poem. Every word is necessary to the argument; every cadence, every suggestion of literary tradition, whether that suggestion occur in the cadence or in the explicit meaning of the words, contributes to the feeling which the argument endeavors to convey; and the theme, though not the greatest conceivable, is a great one.

The language of the poem is essentially abstract, but it is worth our trouble to examine briefly the few references to concrete details. In the first stanza, *mark*, as I understand it, is a target, but we are not expected to visualize a target or shooting at a target or the raising of a target. The terms have receded into almost pure abstraction. In the second stanza, *allay* is, if this is possible, even closer to pure abstraction. The third and fourth stanzas are purely abstract. In the remainder of the poem, *temples, garlands, altars, flame, shrine, spark,* and *kindle* come a little closer to visibility, but the degree of visibility is small and the degree of abstraction is great. If these details were visualized more sharply, they would obstruct the argument, and the poem would be weakened further by the fact that these images, merely as images, would be stereotyped. The argument, however, is not stereotyped, but is original and moving, and these details do not obstruct: rather, they contribute to the feeling communicated by the argument by way of their connotations.

" To Heaven " is a greater poem. For one thing, the subject is greater. For another, the poem depends less heavily upon an antecedent body of poetry; and, although it depends upon an understanding of the Christian religious experience, this is more generally understood, and the poem moves more rapidly and with greater weight of meaning line by line. In other words, the poem is more nearly self-contained.

Good and great God, can I not think of Thee,
But it must, straight, my melancholy be?
Is it interpreted in me disease,
That, laden with my sins, I seek for ease?
O be Thou witness, that the reins dost know
And hearts of all, if I be sad for show;
And judge me after: if I dare pretend
To aught but grace, or aim at other end.
As Thou art all, so be Thou all to me,
First, midst, and last, converted One and Three!
My faith, my hope, my love; and in this state,
My judge, my witness, and my advocate.
Where have I been this while exiled from Thee,
And whither rap'd, now Thou but stoop'st to me?
Dwell, dwell here still! O, being everywhere,
How can I doubt to find Thee ever here?
I know my state, both full of shame and scorn,
Conceived in sin, and unto labor born,
Standing with fear, and must with horror fall,
And destined unto judgment after all.
I feel my griefs too, and there scarce is ground
Upon my flesh t'inflict another wound:
Yet dare I not complain or wish for death,
With holy Paul, lest it be thought the breath
Of discontent; or that these prayers be
For weariness of life, not love of Thee.

This poem deals with a major theme, and there are no crude flaws; yet this could be true and the poem still fall short of mastery. The reasons for the success of the poem are hard to describe, for there is no imagery, no decoration, and the metrical and stanzaic forms employed are the simplest in English. The poem has no faults that I can discover, and faults are always easier to discuss than virtues. The surface is tight and smooth; there is almost no opening.

Yet one can note certain facts, at the risk, perhaps, of seeming pedantic. The rhythmic structure of the line is of the post-Sidneyan variety: that is, the accented syllables (and the unaccented also) vary widely in degree of accentuation, so that the line is flexible and subtle, rather than heavy and emphatic. The cesuras are managed with great skill: they fall most often after the second foot or the third, or in the middle of the third, but in line twenty the cesura falls in the middle of the fourth foot; and in many lines the secondary pauses complicate the cesural structure greatly, for example, in ten, eleven, and twelve, and there are other less obvious examples. The heroic couplet is used in these respects with a skill that one can seldom find equalled within similar limits by Dryden or Pope. The relationship of sentence structure to linear and stanzaic structure is similarly brillant: the closed couplet is the norm, and the first, second, seventh, and eighth couplets are complete units, the last of these containing two closely related sentences, the others one each; the third and fourth couplets, the fifth and sixth, the ninth and tenth, the eleventh and twelfth and thirteenth, are longer units; and within these sentences there is considerable variety of structure regardless of length, this variety affecting not merely the sentence but the rhythm of the line and of the group of lines.

Jonson employs two other common devices in this poem: the play upon words in the eighth couplet (*everywhere* and *ever here*), and the play upon an idea (that of the Trinity) in the fifth and sixth couplets. This kind of ingenuity resulted in some of the best and some of the worst passages in the Renaissance; the ingenuity here seems not only justifiable but inescapable: it is an essential part of the argument.

The series of triads resulting from the concept of the Trinity is especially impressive: it occurs in brief space and rapidly; it is not forced but seems a natural series of comparisons; it speeds the rhythm for a few lines (at a moment when the increased speed is a proper expression of passion); and it varies the rhythm of the whole poem, providing a fine preparation for the slower and more sombre movement of the later lines. It prepares us likewise for the final series of theological statements, which, however, are not arranged in triads—those in couplets nine and ten.

The devices which I have described are simple, when considered in general; their effectiveness, like the effectiveness of that other simple device, good diction, depends upon the fine shades in which they appear in the particular context—these fine shades are among the principal marks of genius. These fine shades of statement, however, could not exist were it not for the clear substance of the poem and the clear organization of the substance. In connection with this clarity—which may appear to some to be simplicity—there is one point which I think it worth while to bring surely to light: the theme of this poem is somewhat less simple than it may appear at first glance. The poem deals with love for God and the desire for death. God is perfect being, and therefore good; life, as the poet knows it, is being, however imperfect, and therefore good as a matter of theory. But Jonson, in middle age, does not fear death, as Shakespeare professes to fear it and as Donne apparently fears it in fact: his temptation is "weariness of life"; his duty, which he accepts with a semi-suppressed despair, is to overcome this weariness. There is a recognition of reality here, distinct from a literary convention (as in Shakespeare) and from a gift for personal drama, or perhaps melodrama (as in Donne), which is very impressive. Much of the power of the poem resides in one of the elementary facts of life: the fact that a middle-aged man of intelligence is often readier to die than to live if he merely indulges his feelings. Jonson deals with the real problem, not with a spurious problem.

These two poems illustrate the qualities which I have been trying to describe; they illustrate a plainness more akin to Gascoigne or Wyatt, or especially to Greville, than to any obvious quality in Sidney; Jonson, like Greville, is one on whom the black ox has trod. But these poems illustrate especially that fine control of nuances of feeling which are possible only to the stylist who deliberately abandons, yet remembers, the obvious graces; such writing is not only more weighty than that of Sidney, but it is more sensitive, more skillful.

Jonson's major poems have been neglected in favor of his minor poems, masterly performances in themselves, but less illustrative both of Jonson's genius and the age. The minor poems carry something over from the old courtly tradition to the new: the courtly element is offered playfully in Jonson and in his disciples of the seventeenth century; it is not offered with the benumbing pretence of seriousness which we find in Sidney and Spenser and others. The minor lyrics, however, with the aid of his plays, other writings, and legendary personality, have been able to keep him in some measure before the student's eye as a lyrical poet; he has never, in this capacity, lapsed into the obscurity in which Raleigh was long permitted to rest and in which Gascoigne and Greville rest to this day. If the reader with fixed habits could wrench his attention to the major poems long enough to appreciate them, this act would not only put him in possession of what is probably one of the two or three greatest bodies of short poems composed in the English Renaissance but would aid him to understand a number of other great poets as well.

Among the lesser of Jonson's poems which should be read

with especial care are these: the epitaphs on his children, especially that on his son; the epitaph on Salathiel (or Salomon) Pavy;
"This morning timely rapt with holy fire" (to the Countess of
Bedford); "A Hymn to God the Father"; the second poem to
Charis; "The Hour Glass"; "My Picture Left in Scotland";
and the song in *Love's Triumph through Callipolis* beginning:
"Joy, joy to mortals the rejoicing fires." There are in addition
the justly famous minor masterpieces such as "Drink to me only
with thine eyes," and "Queen and huntress chaste and fair,"
poems which discipline the heritage of the song books and
bequeath it to the seventeenth century.

IV

During the Renaissance, the style of the short poem is largely
classifiable as ornate or plain, although both elements may occur
in one poem. When sensory detail is employed, it is commonly
in the form of ornament. In certain poems the ornate style is
controlled with a good deal of firmness, but the sensory detail is
nevertheless ornament, something added, something attached.
The poems of the plain style, however, concentrate on the essential theme, and the best of them seem to me the best poems of
the period.

But the plain style sacrifices a part of our experience, the
sensory, and the ornate style does not really recover it in a satisfactory way. We are, of course, rational animals, and most of
our thinking is done in abstractions, and this was going on even
before Plato; and we have become familiar with abstractions
and with their relationships to daily experience—they can be used
with emotional force as well as with intellectual. But we are

also sensory animals, and we live in a physical universe, and if we are blind to the impressiveness and meanings of our physical surroundings, we are limited. It ought to be possible to embody our sensory experience in our poetry in an efficient way, not as ornament, and with no sacrifice of rational intelligence.

In the eighteenth century, poets and theorists of poetry, harking back to Hobbes and Locke, decided that all ideas arise from the association of sense-perceptions. By the end of the century it was often believed that ideas could be expressed in terms of sense-perceptions. This notion is foolish: no matter how ideas may have arisen, they cannot at this late date be equated with the impressions of sense. The notion is, however, precisely the basis of Pound's theory of the image and of the ideogram, and is the central idea in most of the Romantic theories of poetry in the United States, England, France, and other Western countries in the nineteenth and twentieth centuries. Since ideas cannot really be expressed purely in terms of sense-perceptions, we are merely given pure sense-perceptions. We get what Frank Kermode has called the romantic image—that is, the mindless image, the impenetrable image, which seems to mean but in reality merely is.[3] Mallarmé's poetic absolute is a version of this idea. Most of our contemporary poets and critics are operating on one form or another of it. The associationists provided another principle, however—one of structure: instead of the rational structure of the Renaissance, we were offered a structure based on association. Most of Pound's *Cantos* illustrate both of these principles in an extreme form, and in spite of the talent which went into this lifelong experiment, they are far from satisfactory. However, it is possible to employ associative structure without sensory imagery: one finds it in much of the work of Charles Churchill.

[3] *Romantic Image* (Macmillan, New York, 1957).

It is possible also to keep both of these principles under suffi-
ciently strict control to make them very useful, to make them,
in fact, means to enrich the older procedures.

I have already published a brief discussion of controlled associationism in connection with Paul Valéry.[4] I will now say a
few words about it as we find it in Stevens's "Sunday Morning."
However, where the principles of structure and of imagery are
both involved, I think that we have controlled associationism
primarily in the structure. The imagery is post-associationistic.
Let us call the total method post-symbolist.

Stevens, in his best poems, is a master of the resources of
meter and syntax, and of the resources of rhythm that can result
from meter and syntax; and he is a master of diction. These
facts are well known, and I shall waste no time on them; but I
would like to add that in my opinion he is, in these respects,
fully the equal of Ben Jonson and the superior of Donne,
Sidney, or the Shakespeare of the sonnets. What I would like
to discuss briefly is the nature and function of his imagery.

"Sunday Morning" deals primarily with a doctrine that one
can call Paterian hedonism. I have objected to this doctrine
elsewhere, and I will not repeat myself. The poem deals also
with the rejection of Christianity and with the imminence of
death in a universe which is at once infinitely beautiful and
perfectly incomprehensible. It is with this view of the universe
and with certain aspects of man's place in it, as the imagery
is used to express this view, that I am now concerned, and I
shall discuss only a few passages of the poem.

In the first stanza the protagonist

---

[4] *The Function of Criticism: Problems and Exercises* (Alan Swallow,
Denver, 1957), pp. 58–75.

> . . . feels the dark
> Encroachment of that old catastrophe,
> As a calm darkens among water-lights.

The catastrophe I take to be death in general and the death of
Jesus in particular. If one has ever seen a calm darken among
water lights on a large bay or lake, the image is unforgettable.
A few lines farther on, "The day is like wide water without
sound," and the water image is extended. In the next six stanzas
the religious and ethical problems are discussed, and then in the
final stanza we return to the water, which by now has become
more real than figurative:

> She hears upon that water without sound,
> A voice that cries, "The tomb in Palestine
> Is not the porch of spirits lingering.
> It is the grave of Jesus, where he lay."

And then:

> We live in an old chaos of the sun,
> Or old dependency of day and night,
> Or island solitude, unsponsored, free,
> Of that wide water, inescapable.

In the first water image, death encroached as a calm darkens
among water lights; then the day was like water; then infinite
space is water—bright, beautiful, and inscrutable, the home of
life and death. Every phrase in this last passage is beautiful at
the descriptive level, but the descriptive and the philosophical
cannot be separated: *chaos, solitude, unsponsored, free, inescapable*
work at both levels. The sensory detail is not ornament;
it is a part of the essential theme. In the next three lines there
is a measure of separation:

> Deer walk upon our mountains, and the quail

> Whistle about us their spontaneous cries;
> Sweet berries ripen in the wilderness;

Out of context, this is merely description, but fine description. In context, it is a part of what precedes and what follows, but there is only one word which makes a philosophical connection: *spontaneous*. The quail are nonhuman, free, spontaneous: they can be admired but not understood; they are part of the wilderness. The last lines are similar, except that the number of charged words is greater:

> And, in the isolation of the sky,
> At evening, casual flocks of pigeons make
> Ambiguous undulations as they sink
> Downward to darkness on extended wings.

Out of context, these lines are fine description but minor poetry; in context, they are great poetry, and the words responsible are: *isolation, casual, ambiguous*, and *darkness*. Out of context, these words would not be suspected, I imagine, of carrying any real weight of meaning beyond the descriptive meaning. Their significance has been prepared by the total poem, and they sum the poem up.

These pigeons are different from Shakespeare's lark. The lark was merely a lark, with the author's personal sentimentality imposed upon it arbitrarily. The pigeons embody an idea as well as a feeling, and the idea motivates the feeling. The pigeons cannot be separated from the idea: they are a part of the universe which the poet is trying to understand, and at this point they are an efficiently representative part. The rational soul and the sensible soul are united: we do not have the purely rational soul of Jonson or the purely sensible soul of Pound; and there is no decoration. The universe which Stevens describes is ambiguous in its ultimate meanings, but there is nothing ambiguous in the style: ambiguity is rendered with the greatest of precision. And the universe is one which we can recognize as our own, even if we disagree with Stevens's philosophy. The physical details are not ingenious set pieces; we know where we are.

There is more to the art of poetry than a kind of imagery or the lack of imagery. As I have said, we must have an important theme, an understanding of the theme which is in some measure defensible, and a command of syntax, meter, rhythm, and diction; and one will not come by these simple-sounding acquisitions without both genius and education. But the post-symbolist sensibility, other things being equal, seems to me potentially the greatest achievement in occidental poetry. One can find examples of it earlier: in Emily Dickinson and F. G. Tuckerman, and occasionally, perhaps, in Baudelaire and in Leconte de Lisle; but it emerges most clearly in Valéry and Stevens. I doubt that either of these men understood the implications of the style of his best work. Neither was a scholar, and the theoretical statements of both are confused. Both were caught in an historical movement which they understood imperfectly. But they had sufficient genius to make the most of their immediate background in a few poems. The poems are there to be understood, and if we can understand them, we may well be at the beginning of the greatest poetical movement that we have known.

Marianne Moore

Dame

Edith

Sitwell

GREAT IN FAR GREATER WAYS, DAME Edith Sitwell is a virtuoso of rhythm and accent. She has given me immense pleasure, intensifying my interest in rhythm, and has also encouraged me in my rhythmic eccentricities. I can scarcely read the Bible without forsaking content for rhythm, as where the Apostle Paul speaks of the shipwreck on Malta and says, " when the ship could no longer bear up into the wind, we let her drive." " Let her drive " is a better rhythm, is it not, than we have in the new version, which reads " and were driven? " " When we could not face the wind, we gave way to it and were driven."

Façade was apprenticeship, Dame Edith, or Miss Sitwell as she was then, insists, but an apprenticeship of great virtuosity; and of wit as in " The Higher Sensualism " when Queen Circe said

> " Young man, I will buy
> Your plumaged coat for my pig to try—
>
> Then with angels he'll go a-dancing hence
> From sensuality into sense! "

"I used to practice writing," Dame Edith says, "as a pianist practices music." She says that she would take a waltz or a polka or the music of the barrel organ beneath her window and translate it into words, just as she has done in the phrase from this "Country Dance."

> But Silenus
> Has seen us.

Dame Edith then explored the nature of the long line and its possibilities. William Carlos Williams has said in his book *I Wanted to Write a Poem*, "I found I could not use the long line because of my nervous nature." An adagio, moreover, "is hard to sustain at concert pitch," as *The Times Literary Supplement* has said. We have it, however, when Edith Sitwell writes

> archipelagoes
> Of stars and young thin moons from great wings falling
> As ripples widen.

How pleasing, her dactyls: *porphyry, basicilica, Babylyn*; and *babioun* (*babioun* borrowed from Ben Jonson, as she says). How neat, the rhyme "Noctambulo" with "folio":

> The public scribe, Noctambulo
> Where moonlight, cold as blades of grass
> Echoes upon deserted walls,
> Turned his dusty folio;

and this: "old Bacchantes black with wine, / Whose very hair has changed into a vine." We have here, I think, something of the automatic self-initiated effect of Leslie Brooke's "Johnny Crow's Party":

> The snake
> Got entangled
> With the rake.

> The sheep
> Fell asleep
> And the armadillo
> Used him as a pillow.

Dame Edith's irregularities in set meter are hyper-skilful, as when she creates a pause after *any* in "anybody"—in "Mary Stuart to James Bothwell" (Casket Letter No. 2):

> Leaving you, I was sundered like the sea!
> Departed from the place where I left my heart
> I was as small as any body may be.

That is to say, any *body*, with the accent on body.

There is no melody in Pope, Dame Edith says, because there is no irregularity. "To have melody, there must be variations in the outward structure." An expert of the condensed phrase, she also says, "I try to make my images exact"; and does she not as in the word "sundered" and by inventing "donkey's hide-grass" for the beast of the attorney? ·

> O'er donkey's hide-grass the attorney
> Still continues on his journey.

In the opening lines of "The Sleeping Beauty," the incantatory effect of the whole passage is a metaphor creating a sense, I think, of deep, mysterious, fairyworld remoteness:

> When we come to that dark house,
> Never sound of wave shall rouse
> The bird that sings within the blood
> Of those who sleep in that deep wood.

Dame Edith reminds Katherine Anne Porter of Lully, Rameau, Monteverdi, and Purcell, of old courtly music, weddings, christenings, great crystal-lighted banquets, in sweet-smelling gardens under the full moon. Generalizing, she says, "There is no finer sight than to see an artist growing great." Sir George Sitwell, Dame Edith's father, said, "Edith will commit suicide when she finds she cannot write poetry." A need for this has not arisen.

One cannot, of course, exhibit virtuosity without being deplored and combatted. As Mr. Henry McBride—art critic for *The Dial*, the New York *Sun*, and *The Art News*—has said, "One may judge the vitality of an artist by the extent to which he is resisted." Dame Edith recalls that certain lines of hers once received "a mingling of bouquets and brickbats—with a strong predominance of brickbats"; yet invariably, as *The New Statesman and Nation* said on June 23, 1954, "losing every battle, she won the campaign"; in fact, "emerged more majestic, more unaccountably modern than ever."

In *Façade* she said that it was necessary to find heightened expression for the heightened speed of our time. However, she added "in spite of the fact that the rhythms which I practised in *Façade* were heightened, concentrated, and frequently more violent than those of the poets who had preceded us immediately, it was supposed by many that I had *discarded* rhythm. But we must not complain if the patterns in our mundane works are not perceived by the unobservant," this allusion being to Bishop Burnet, who had found fault with the constellations and said, if only the stars had been composed "according to the rules of art and symmetry."

Some readers may regard a word of Dame Edith's as arbitrary, or a statement may be termed "a shade oracular." In her choice of words, she is to herself always justified. "Neatness of execution is essential to sublimity," she says; and she indeed improves DeQuincey when she considers language an "incarnation" of thought rather than "the dress of thought." She is instructively "neat" in revising her own work; in substitutions, for instance, of a general term for a specific in her "Metamorphosis."

> When first the dew with golden foot
> Makes tremble every leaf and strawberry root.

This is made to read in the second version of 1946:

> Here once in Spring, the dew with golden foot
> Made tremble every leaf and hidden root.

When she exhibits other authors—Christopher Smart, for instance, in her early three volume anthology, and when in *The Book of the Winter* she selects examples from Herrick, Blake, and Donne—her wand is tipped with a diamond. Of compiling *The Book of the Winter*, Dame Edith said, "I was not concerned with producing a hodge-podge of everything that has been written about winter. . . . One of the greatest difficulties encountered in making an anthology of this kind is to resign oneself to omissions. I have had to exclude many beauties because they pulled the pattern out of shape." From Donne, it is not complementary spectacular matched lines of verse which she quoted, but this passage from a sermon preached by Donne in April, 1629: "The root of all is God, but it is not the way to receive fruits to dig at the root but to reach to the boughs." For Dylan Thomas, we have this all-encompassing apologia: "His love for those who have received no mercies from life is great." *The Book of the Winter* is marked by fire and novelty throughout, as in Sir Thomas Browne's "Of Crystals and Icicles"; and in this apparition or vision from *I Live under a Black Sun*—Dame Edith's novel: "A figure would shine through the night, circling swiftly as if it were a swallow, or floating, a black swan on the wide water-black marble pavements; . . . Rag Castle after rag castle, the world of beggars was swept along, and night fell upon the two nations, the rich and the poor, who alone inhabit the earth." Here are prototypes of Lazarus and Dives, made so emphatic in Dame Sitwell's later work. Tom O' Bedlam (anonymous), quoted only in part, perhaps epitomizes the contagion of the whole book:

> While I do sing,
> "Any food, any feeding,
> Feeding, drink, or clothing,"
> Come dame or maid
> Be not afraid
> Poor Tom will injure nothing.
>
> The meek, the wise, the gentle
> Me handle, touch, and spare not;
> But those that cross
> Tom Rhinoceros
> Do what the panther dare not.
>
> .   .   .   .   .
>
> With an host of furious fancies,
> Whereof I am commander,
> With a burning Speare, and a horse of aire,
> To the wildernesse I wander.

In his Introduction to Paul Valéry's *The Art of Poetry*, T. S. Eliot says, seemingly as an afterthought, " How Poetry is related to life, Valéry does not say." My own thought here, may be at a tangent from the query which Mr. Eliot may imply; but for me there is immediacy in Edith Sitwell's statement: " The behaviour of the world affects our beliefs and incites the mind to tumult to speak as a Cassandra or as an elegist." Her "awareness of the potentialities of atomic research," as a press commentator has said, "make more emphatic her assurance of the spiritual power behind the material façade." Reflecting current thought—or so I hope—Robert Frost has simplified the matter

of why we write when he says, " It is what every poem is about—
how the spirit is to surmount the material pressure upon us."

In our battle with the material world, does not Edith Sitwell
rise to bear humanity aid? " As for the poet taking an interest in
his fellow human being," she says, " he is a brother speaking to
a brother . . . supporting his brother's flagging footsteps." Over-
powered by a sense of the Universal Cain, of brother as murderer
of brother, of the chaingang sentenced to ninety-nine years, she
says, " I come to testify." And of her testimony, W. B. Yeats
said, " Something absent from all literature was back again,
passion ennobled by intensity, by endurance, by wisdom."

" With what are these on fire? " she asks, " with passion, Hate,
Infatuation, and old age, and death
With sorrow, longing, and with laboring breath."

Time (December 26, 1955) said, " she writes for the sake of
sound, of color, and from an awareness of God and regard for
man." She herself says, " All great poetry is dipped in the dyes
of the heart," and quoting perhaps from Whitman, " all things
are in the clime of man's forgiveness." As one thinks of her
poetry, who could lament, as the *London Times Literary Supplement* says certain poets do, " our lack of the large theme and
forcible expression of it? " " To what ideals would I reach in my
poetry? " Dame Edith asks. " How far I am from these no one
could see more clearly than I. Technically, I would come to a
vital language—each word possessing an infinite power of germi-
nation. Spiritually to give holiness to each common day." By
reason of her humility and her compassion—I would not qualify
it—she cages conviction.

Mark Van Doren

The Poems of

Thomas Hardy

A TEXT FOR ANY DISCUSSION OF Thomas Hardy's poems might be the 373rd Pensée of Pascal: "I shall here write my thoughts without order, and not perhaps in unintentional confusion; that is true order, which will always indicate my object by its very disorder. I should do too much honor to my subject if I treated it with order, since I want to show that it is incapable of it." Pascal's subject, to be sure, was not anybody's poems; it was everybody's life; it was the whole of experience as he tried to grasp it. Yet the text has a peculiar fitness in Hardy's case, for it can be made to refer not merely to the overwhelming volume and variety of his poetic output but to the view he himself took of the world; or the views, for there were many of these, and he never pretended that they were consistent with one another.

In one of his prefaces he confessed how difficult it had been to arrange the present poems in anything like a natural or rational order. Indeed, it was impossible, and so he had given up. "I mean," he said, "the chance little shocks that may be caused

. . . by the juxtaposition of unrelated, even discordant, effusions; poems perhaps years apart in the making, yet facing each other. . . . But the difficulties of arranging the themes in a graduated kinship of moods would have been so great that irrelation was almost unavoidable with efforts so diverse. I must trust for right note-catching to those finely-touched spirits who can divine without half a whisper, whose intuitiveness is proof against all the accidents of inconsequence." The problem, familiar of course to any poet, must have been particularly torturous for Hardy, who had been prolific for so long. The eight volumes of short poems he published between 1898 and 1928—between, that is, his fifty-eighth and his eighty-eighth years—contained by no means all new matter. He was always bringing forward poems he had written in the 1860's, or in any of the three subsequent decades; for he started as as poet, and only because he could not get published in that capacity had he written novels. Now that he was determined to be known as a poet and nothing but a poet he ransacked his desk for "effusions" that might still do. No wonder he found it difficult to arrange the result.

The modern reader cannot do so either; nor can the modern critic decide with readiness which poems of Hardy's are the best, let alone the most characteristic. No poet more stubbornly resists selection. And this has not been to Hardy's advantage in the field where reputations are made. There is no core of pieces, no inner set of classic or perfect poems, which would prove his rank. Perhaps no poem of Hardy's is perfect; indeed, there is no great poet in whom imperfection is easier to find. Yet he is a great poet, and there are those who love him without limit even though they will admit his thousand failures and defects. With such persons it is the whole of him that registers and counts; one thing they would be reluctant to admit, namely, that out of his *Collected Poems* a *Selected Poems* might be put together which would contain everything pertaining to his essence. His essence, they would insist, is everywhere in the body of his work: in the capillaries, the tissues, no less than in the sinews and the heart. For them, in other words, the *Collected Poems* is neither too long nor too miscellaneous; its reputation with them depends upon the very richness that puts other readers off. They have made the effort the volume requires, and the reward of that effort is their knowledge of a poet who is great even when he is not writing well. He is great in himself, as one who thinks, feels, sees, and speaks; and he cannot lose their allegiance.

This miracle is worked in the *Collected Poems* alone; not in the slight verse play, *The Famous Tragedy of the Queen of Cornwall,* nor even in that more impressive drama in one-hundred and thirty scenes, *The Dynasts.* It is good to have read *The Dynasts* once, for it contains curious and wonderful things; but few can have read it twice, at least all the way through. It does not get close to its people, whom Hardy too convincingly calls automata, cheese-mites, and mackerel. The view he takes of them is from too far away. This of course is the view he wants to take, since a theory rules him as he writes: a theory not unlike that of Tolstoy as he wrote *War and Peace* on the same subject, the wars of Napoleon. For neither man did individuals count, at any rate so far as theory went: there was no such thing as character or will, there was only mass movement, and even in this movement there was no meaning. But Tolstoy so far forgot his theory as to create Natasha, Andrey, and Pierre, to name only three out of dozens of souls to whom his pen gave life; whereas Hardy, with that stubbornness which his admirers will always forgive him, refused to budge from the platform he had

erected whereon to stand and state his thesis—the calamity of
Napoleon was fortuitous, without design or moral, nor were
the sufferings of innumerable men so much as noted by the
Immanent Will whose unfeeling mind worked

> unconsciously, as heretofore,
> Eternal artistries in Circumstance.

The Spirits with whom Hardy shares his platform, bodiless
beings who have no more control over the drama than he has,
say magnificent things in a monotone their poet never violates;
but they say what he chooses to have them say, since they are
nothing but spokesmen for his metaphysics. When we descend
into the action—battles, conferences, love passages, riots, and
duels—we do not find ourselves among people to whom warmth
has even by inadvertence been given. Nor do these people speak
fine verse, as often the Spirits do; they are not enough alive for
that, nor does Hardy wish them to be. He has been more eloquent in his stage-directions; it is to those that the reader is most
likely to return. For example, this early one:

> The nether sky opens, and Europe is disclosed as a prone
> and emaciated figure, the Alps shaping like a backbone, and
> the branching mountain-chains like ribs, the peninsular pla-
> teau of Spain forming a head. Broad and lengthy lowlands
> stretch from the north of France across Russia like a grey-
> green garment hemmed by the Ural mountains and the glis-
> tening Arctic Ocean.
>
> The point of view then sinks downward through space,
> and draws near to the surface of the perturbed countries,
> where the peoples, distressed by events which they did not
> cause, are seen writhing, heaving, and vibrating in their
> various cities and nationalities.

That is eloquent, surely; indeed, it is brilliant; but it closes a door on drama which is something like the door of a tomb. Those of us who insist on entering must abandon all hope of making human sense out of what we see.

No, it is the *Collected Poems* upon which Hardy's reputation will be obliged to rest. And this is a volume, as has already been hinted, in which a traveller can lose his way. Its contents are a cavern the quality of whose darkness is always changing, and the number of whose recesses appears to increase as the explorer stumbles on. Lights gleam and then subside, only to be lit again in further corners. The reader, that is to say, is forever making new discoveries: either of Hardy or of himself. If of Hardy, they have to do with dimensions of his thought and feeling not previously observed. If of himself, they have to do with certain poems he seems to be reading for the first time; or reading with a sense of power in them that startles him, for there had been no sign of it before. No poet has so changeable a surface as Hardy, no poet maintains in his reader so changeable a mind. Which are his best poems, and which are his worst? The question never seems to get settled; no wonder he becomes the anthologist's despair.

Hardy himself has been before us in the cavern, lighting candles that would seem to show the way. Only, they do not show it all. They show, in fact, only their own wicks and tallow. They are the "philosophical" poems in which Hardy states his theory of life. It is the same theory that he states in *The Dynasts*, and it is equally unilluminating of anything save his own conscious thought. They are good poems, but they are not the ones that move us to call him a great poet. We want more from a poet than a theory of life; we want, if such a thing is possible, the look, feel, sound, taste, and even smell of life itself. And that is what Hardy eventually provides, and provides so richly

that his name is sure to last. Meanwhile there are these philosophical poems which tell us that he finds no intelligibility in
events, no form or order in the world. They are such poems as
only he could write; they say what they have to say in his own
idiom, for he meant very personally what he said in them; and
they make a solemn, piercing music which alone would certify
their sincerity. But they are not the heart of the book as he
must have supposed they would be. They take their place among
the thinner tissues, the ones with the least blood in them.

The heart of the book, assuming it can be located at all, is
older and tougher than these poems are. The book was not a
single effort like *The Dynasts*, conceived and carried through
with little or no interruption; it was the work of almost seventy
years, and Hardy himself changed much in all that time. Or if
he did not change, he submitted himself to many chances, and
caught on the fly a bewildering number of perceptions which in
the nature of things could not have been alike. An assiduous
taker of notes upon himself, he rendered on a wide front his
experience of the world, so that there is scarcely anything he
has not understood and said before he is finished. This is not
precisely to say that the rest of the book contradicts or denies
the philosophical poems. Rather, it absorbs them; it finds a place
for them and leaves them there.

In that place they say the same thing over and over: nature
and man have come to a misunderstanding, and this misunderstanding will never be cured. Nature—sometimes the term is
God—did not make man to think and feel; man was once unconscious, as other things still are, as mildews and mandrakes
are, as stones and birds. That was the good time, when suffering
of course existed yet could not tell itself it did; when no creature
expected more than it could get; when the " disease of feeling "

and the malady of thought had not yet been born in the brain of one creature, man, who now is doomed to pain by the very fact of this monstrous birth. The qualities we think distinguish us are the qualities that make us miserable. We long for what we can never have, just as we agonize over losses and failures of which nature takes only routine account.

If we could be one with nature again, as Lucretius thought we could, and as Naturalism says we must, we might recover that happiness of which we were unconscious when we had it; but this can never be. The gulf between us and our maker widens with every idea we have, and with every refinement of experience. Nature remains the same; we change, and in the process move away from her into a loneliness for which there is no remedy. The more we use our minds, the less we understand; yet we must keep on using our minds, as we must keep on hoping and despairing. Even nature is aware of all this, and laments her wayward child; though the only thing she can tell us is that if we came back to her we would be coming back to unconsciousness, we would be as toads and stars, as mushrooms and meteors.

> Maybe now
> Normal unawareness waits rebirth.

So in his last book, *Winter Words*, Hardy dares to hope; but it is the dimmest hope, and of the dimmest thing.

No wonder Hardy calls himself a tragic poet, and says on one occasion: "Comedy lies." No wonder he is at home with gloom, which he certainly is; or that he can note as a scientist would some signs that the world, like any other machine, is running down. In an uncanny poem, "Nature's Questioning," he even endows inanimate objects with the power to wonder what men wonder:

When I look forth at dawning, pool,
    Field, flock, and lonely tree,
    All seem to gaze at me
Like chastened children sitting silent in a school;

Their faces dulled, constrained, and worn,
    As though the master's ways
    Through the long teaching days
Had cowed them till their early zest was overborne.

Upon them stirs in lippings mere
    (As if once clear in call,
    But now scarce breathed at all)—
"We wonder, ever wonder, why we find us here!

"Has some vast Imbecility,
    Mighty to build and blend,
    But impotent to tend,
Framed us in jest, and left us now to hazardry?

"Or come we of an Automaton
    Unconscious of our pains? . . .
    Or are we live remains
Of Godhead dying downwards, brain and eye now gone?"

These are terrible questions, put with a terrible candor, which
of course is Hardy's. There is one further question, more difficult for Hardy to phrase because it seems to him rhetorical:

"Or is it that some high Plan betides,
    As yet not understood,
    Of Evil stormed by Good,
We the Forlorn Hope over which Achievement strides?"

He phrases it rather stuffily; he is not convinced that it was
worth asking; but·then he closes with music—his music—on the
note most native to him:

Thus things around. No answerer I . . .
    Meanwhile the winds, and rains,

And Earth's old glooms and pains
Are still the same, and Life and Death are neighbors nigh.

"Are still the same." Perhaps the heart of Hardy is just there. Winds and rains, and glooms and pains—those are the matter out of which he makes his art; they are the very folklore of his life, the familiar data, never to disappear, over which his imagination can pore without becoming tired. He would not know what to do without them; and once he said as much, in the poem he wrote refusing an invitation to the United States. Our claim to be young and happy was precisely what kept him away:

> I shrink to seek a modern coast
> Whose riper times have yet to be;
> Where the new regions claim them free
> From that long drip of human tears
> Which peoples old in tragedy
> Have left upon the centuried years.

No, he must remain where men, bent under pressures unimaginable in a new world, were all but deformed by pain and failure. His allegiance was to irony: to the monstrous coincidence, the ghastly event, or else—reducing calamity's scale—to the queer outcome, the miniature misadventure, the misery no bigger than a mouse. It was characteristic of Hardy that his poem about the sinking of the *Titanic* dealt with only one fact: the building of the iceberg and the building of the ship at whatever moment in each case would bring it about that the two collided when and where they did. But it was just as characteristic of him that he should write, in "The Sun on the Letter," about the odd circumstance that sunlight played as brightly over bad news as it would have over good. The size of things did not matter to him so long as all of them, huge or minute, testified to the principle of chance—or, as he put it in an early poem,

Hap. Crass Casualty was still another name for it. And in nature as men once knew her it would not have been noticed, since nothing would have been noticed. It is the disease of feeling that has made men hypersensitive to truth: they cannot take what must be and what is. They are skinless creatures, shivering in the winds of circumstance.

Now it might follow from the firmness with which Hardy held on to this view that he would have no sympathy with those who feel; that he would spend all of his strength, as Lucretius did, in lecturing them upon the absurdity of their error; that he would, in other words, be cold and heartless. The contrary, as any reader of him knows, is true. In all the world there is no more feeling poet. He proves it in a hundred ways, no one of which is logically defensible; has he not demonstrated, even to monotony, the foolishness of tears? It is now that the great poet emerges, the poet whose humanity is profounder than his thought. He is that most moving kind of man, the kind that tries not to feel yet does; he is that most convincing of lovers, the one who begins by thinking he does not believe in love. Hardy should scorn the emotions of himself and others; instead of which, he lets them break his heart.

The intensity of his concern may show itself in bizarre, unlikely ways, but there is no mistaking the intensity, as for example in "The Head Above the Fog," which gives life to a mistress in the very act of decapitating her:

> Something do I see
> Above the fog that sheets the mead,
> A figure like to life indeed,
> Moving along with spectre-speed,
>   Seen by none but me.
>
>   O the vision keen!—

Tripping along to me for love
As in the flesh it used to move,
Only its hat and plume above
   The evening fog-fleece seen.

  In the day-fall wan,
When nighted birds break off their song,
Mere ghostly head it skims along,
Just as it did when warm and strong,
   Body seeming gone.

  Such it is I see
Above the fog that sheets the mead—
Yea, that which once could breathe and plead!—
Skimming along with spectre-speed
   To a last tryst with me.

The intensity in this case is not Hardy's, it is the ghost's, and the skimming speed of the ghost is what conveys it to us. Hardy is never without the power, indispensable in any ambitious poet, to endow his creations with an energy that seems to be their own. It is he who speaks, but it is they who have the final word. "The Head Above the Fog" treats of a tryst: a favorite subject with Hardy, for nothing interests him more than meetings between lovers; the most moving number for him is two. The meetings are more often sad than successful, but no matter; his deepest sympathies are engaged, and there is always something beautiful in that depth. He may or may not be recording a personal experience; most of the time, he tells us in his prefaces, he is not. It is clear enough that twenty-one poems in *Satires of Circumstance* have to do with the death of his first wife, with whom he had lived thirty-eight years; and these poems are not to be matched in all the literature of grief. Usually, however, we are willing to assume that he is dramatic, or as he himself liked to say, "personative." Whether or not the rule applies to the poem *Near Lanivet, 1872*, we could no more take it for unreal than we could so take *Othello* or *King Lear*.

There was a stunted handpost just on the crest,
    Only a few feet high:
She was tired, and we stopped in the twilight-time
        for her rest,
    At the crossroads close thereby.

She leant back, being so weary, against its stem,
    And laid her arms on its own,
Each open palm stretched out to each end of them,
    Her sad face sideways thrown.

Her white-clothed form at this dim-lit cease of day
    Made her look as one crucified
In my gaze at her from the midst of the dusty way,
    And hurriedly "Don't," I cried.

I do not think she heard. Loosing thence she said,
    As she stepped forth ready to go,
"I am rested now.—Something strange came into my head;
    I wish I had not leant so!"

And wordless we moved onward down from the hill
    In the west cloud's murked obscure,
And looking back we could see the handpost still
    In the solitude of the moor.

"It struck her too," I thought, for as if afraid
    She heavily breathed as we trailed;
Till she said, "I did not think how 'twould look in
        the shade,
    When I leant there like one nailed."

I, lightly: "There's nothing in it. For *you*, anyhow!"
    —"O I know there is not," said she . . .
"Yet I wonder. . . . If no one is bodily crucified now,
    In spirit one may be!"

And we dragged on and on, while we seemed to see
    In the running of Time's far glass
Her crucified, as she had wondered if she might be
    Some day.—Alas, alas!

His lovers are sometimes faithful, sometimes faithless; though as often as not the faithless onces are merely feeble of purpose, perhaps for a reason they cannot understand—they change, and are bewildered by the change. If they are cruel, it may be unintentionally so, or else they remain unaware that they were cruel. "A Maiden's Pledge" is the song of an absolutely faithful girl who will continue so even if her lover never hints of marriage:

Your comet-comings I will wait
With patience time shall not wear through.

Hardy takes pleasure in that, as in one of his best-known songs, "Let Me Enjoy," he says he takes pleasure in countless sweet things that are not for him.

Let me enjoy the earth no less
Because the all-enacting Might
That fashioned forth its loveliness
Had other aims than my delight. . . .

From manuscripts of moving song
Inspired by scenes and dreams unknown,
I'll pour out raptures that belong
To others, as they were my own.

His singular devotion to birds—one could almost say, his obsession with them—has something like this for its source. The intensity of birds, equal to his own, caught him up in their ecstasies as they sang or sported; or suffered, for he had no defenses against the spectacle of one in pain, particularly such a one as he addresses in "The Blinded Bird." His rage against men who run red-hot needles through the eyes of songbirds to increase the sweetness of their voices is stated only by indirection, yet the rage is strong enough:

> Who hath charity? This bird.
> Who suffereth long and is kind,
> Is not provoked, though blind
> And alive ensepulchred?
> Who hopeth, endureth all things?
> Who thinketh no evil, but sings?
> Who is divine? This bird.

For Hardy, it would seem, birds were omens: they had been sent to tell him something. In "The Darkling Thrush" the message is that hope may have some meaning after all, for this bird if not for him. But another thrush, seen out of his window on Christmas day, told him something else again:

> There, to reach a rotting berry,
> Toils a thrush,—constrained to very
> Dregs of food by sharp distress,
> Taking such with thankfulness.
>
> Why, O starving bird, when I
> One day's joy would justify,
> And put misery out of view,
> Did you make me notice you?

Hardy never ceases to take testimony, to read the world as if it were a book, now closed, now open, with too many pages in it ever to let him finish. A tree in London can strike pity out of him because it is not in the country where it belongs. But sometimes it is he who is being read, as in the case of the fallow deer that looked in upon him one night:

We do not discern those eyes
   Watching in the snow;
Lit by lamps of rosy dyes
We do not discern those eyes
   Wondering, aglow,
   Fourfooted, tiptoe.

A poet's power to feel is best proved in the stories he tells, provided he can tell stories. Hardy could; that was where his genius lay; and so it may be that the heart of the *Collected Poems* beats in the narratives that throng it like so many persons, each one of them powerful in his or her own right. The final richness, perhaps, is here. Hardy is the envy of those who would be infinitely fertile in narrative ideas if only they could; it would seem to have been easy for him to be just that. Doubtless he worked harder than appears; there is evidence that he scoured newspapers for material, and took copious notes on stories he overheard in his native Wessex. The appearance, nevertheless, is of a fountain that cannot stop flowing; and its waters are strong waters that thrust forth from deep places. Hardy's stories are little melodramas, sensational, unrelenting, and if need be mournful beyond bearing, as the great ballads are.

In "The Burghers" a man who has planned to ambush his wife and her lover—to kill them with two strokes of his sword as they flee from his house—brings them home with him instead and heaps gifts upon them, of clothes and jewels; then he lets them go, knowing that his kindness to them is a wound which will never heal. In "Her Death and After" a dying wife tells her former lover that she wishes the child she has just borne were his; her husband is not kind to her, and she fears for the child's future, for it is lame. The lover haunts her tomb until it becomes noticeable that he does; the husband himself notices it, and comes to ask him why; then without premeditation he tells the husband that the lame child is his. The child is sent to him and he brings it up, happily because this is what the dead woman would have wished, unhappily because he has hurt her name.

In "The Dance at the Phoenix" a woman of sixty who in her youth had been free with her favors, especially to "sundry troopers of the King's Own Cavalry," is now the virtuous wife of a gentle fellow who knows nothing of this past; and she would have died peacefully in good time had not on a certain evening the King's Cavalry come to the Phoenix Inn for a dance like those of the old days. Jenny, sleeping by her husband, hears the music and cannot refrain from slipping away to join the merriment, old as she is. She dances all night; is escorted home; slips back into bed; and dies of exhaustion which her husband attributes to some natural cause—"The King's said not a word." In "A Sunday Morning Tragedy" a mother tells how, having failed to persuade her daughter's lover that he should marry her because she is with child by him, procures from an herb woman a drug that will dispose of the child; only after she has administered the drug does she hear that the lover, repenting, has published the banns in church; but it is too late, for the drug proves fatal to the daughter. In "The Noble Lady's Tale" the lady's husband, an actor who has given up the stage to please her father, begs her for permission to go back and play for just one night; she consents; he goes, but when he is home again he accuses her of having followed him to the theater, nor does he believe her oaths to the contrary; he finally decides that her wraith had followed him rather than herself in flesh and blood; but this distresses him quite as much, since it suggests that she had not trusted him; he wastes away, and so does she, unable to be sure whether a projection of her had pursued him; yet those who listen to her tale are left with further questions:

> Did she, we wonder, follow
> Jealously?
> And were those protests hollow?—
> Or saw he
> Some semblant dame? Or can wraiths really be?

In "The Moth-Signal" a woman, sitting with her husband one night, tells him she pities a moth that is burning in the candle flame; she goes outdoors to see how the weather is, and her lover comes to her from a tumulus nearby; he remarks that the moth she put out of the window is "burnt and broken," as he is, for he has shattered his own marriage vows; and an ancient Briton speaks from the tumulus, saying people are what they used to be. In "The Sacrilege" a woman of the roads promises her lover that she will go no more to meet his rival, Wrestler Joe, provided he will steal treasure from the cathedral shrine with which she can buy ear-drops and rings; the lover sets off to do this, but only after engaging his brother to murder her in the event that the theft is traced to him (whereupon he will be hanged) and she then takes up with Wrestler Joe; things do go that way, and the brother drowns the woman, whose screams as she dies he will never cease to hear.

In a companion story, "A Trampwoman's Tragedy," the heroine pretends, for no reason she can understand in the sequel, that the child she carries is the child not of her "fancy-man" but of "Jeering John," his rival. Her fancy-man stabs Jeering John to death; is hanged; and leaves the woman wondering why she had done such a mad thing; her only comfort being that she can reassure the ghost of her lover whenever it appears and pleads to be told the truth. In "The Statue of Liberty" a man is asked why he scrubs with mop and water the statue that stands in a city square; his answer is not that he is paid by the city guardians to do it, or that he loves liberty, which the statue symbolizes; it is simply that his daughter was the sculptor's model, and that she had died in this city, distant from his, before he could visit her; what he does now is the only favor he can do his darling, whose good name he thus preserves; but he does not know that he is speaking to the sculptor himself, and that the sculptor knows what happened to the daughter—she died " in the dens of vice." And so on. The list seems to be endless, for Hardy's narrative vein never runs out.

Now and then there is a hearty, humorous tale, since Hardy had that in him too: " The Bride-Night Fire," or " The Home-coming," the latter with a fine refrain:

> Gruffly growled the wind on Toller downland broad and bare,
> And lonesome was the house, and dark; and few came there.

But the prevailing tone is sombre, and the accidents of love or hate, of innocence or guilt, are lighted by an artist in the wings who knows everything about shades and shadows.

He knows everything about time as well. Not only do his stories happen, as all stories do, in time; time is also his very subject. No poet has known better how to move forward and backward in this strangest of dimensions. The poem " One We Knew" concerns an old woman whose memories were pictures for others to study as well as herself:

> She said she had often heard the gibbet creaking
>   As it swayed in the lightning flash,
> Had caught from the neighboring town a small child's shrieking
>   At the cart-tail under the lash. . . .
>
> With cap-framed face and long gaze into the embers—
>   We seated around her knees—

She would dwell on such dead themes, not as one who remembers,
   But as one who sees.

She resembled Hardy in that, for his own memories were like
things printed on a wall; anything that had happened to him,
or had happened to his imagination, was real as present things
were unable to be. He lived in his own gallery of paintings;
nor could he be sure how many of the figures there were ghosts.
This philosopher who prided himself upon his hardness of mind
saw ghosts; he had no business to, but he did. They were the
spirits of murdered persons, or of persons otherwise wronged; but
then too they could be of the mildest sort, like those in " The
Garden Seat":

> At night when reddest flowers are black
> Those who once sat thereon come back;
> Quite a row of them sitting there,
> Quite a row of them sitting there.
>
> With them the seat does not break down,
> Nor winter freeze them, nor floods drown,
> For they are light as upper air,
> They are as light as upper air!

Perhaps the most touching of them all is in the tale of the dead
sailor's mother who comes nightly to the house where she used
to live and waits for her son to appear; it is the only house he
remembers, and so is the only one he can haunt.

Old houses interest anybody, but for Hardy they were tombs
in which time was buried. But buried as it were alive, so that it
moved there, and even spoke or sang there, like one of his
authentic ghosts. An old mirror, he assumed, must be haunted
by the images that had been made upon it; one of his poems,
" The Cheval-Glass," tells of a man who bought at an auction
the mirror before which a woman he once had loved stood

nightly and brushed her hair; he said he saw her in it still, and would keep it with him till he died. Old furniture must remember, Hardy thought, the people who had used it; indeed it must reflect them:

> Hands upon hands, growing paler and paler,
>> As in a mirror a candle-flame
> Shows images of itself, each frailer
>> As it recedes, though the eye may frame
>> Its shape the same.

There was not too much difference for Hardy between an old English house and a prehistoric tumulus or barrow, or a Roman ruin: those had been houses too, if only for bones. The bones still slept there; they even dreamed, and he could hear them talking in their sleep. But the official antiquities of his island were really no older for him than things he himself had seen or done long years ago. Time, that relative thing, was so relative in his case that a certain Roman road on which as a child he had walked with his mother was ancient to him rather for that reason than for the reason that helmed legionaries once marched along it. His imagination had always a temporal cast. His genius could endow things with age that had none otherwise, just as it could read into a single moment, recollected and reconsidered, eternities of meaning which as it passed had not been recognized; the present moment, he is always saying, contains all time and more, but nobody knows this then. Railway trains and stations, for all their bleakness, which he never minimizes, take on in his poems the dignity of timeless crossroads where anything on earth can happen, or anything in hell or heaven.

His love of music is chiefly the love of country singing—old singing, of songs and hymns not much remembered now. His poems ring with the quaint names of former tunes, just as they shake with the feet of dancers: not merely her of the Phoenix Inn, but countless young and old performers of forgotten steps. Church choirs, and groups of warblers by night, serenading bridegrooms or celebrating births and deaths—these have a peculiar, almost a sacred importance for Hardy, who knows the names of ancient instruments, too, and is learned in the folklore of bells. One of his best stories, "The Chapel-Organist," deals with a woman who would rather die than cease to play

> Old Hundredth, Saint Stephen's,
> Mount Zion, New Sabbath, Miles-Lane, Holy Rest, and Arabia,
> and Eaton.

And the whole subject comes perfectly into focus as he watches some young girls in a winter street singing songs whose origins are venerable beyond their comprehension:

> Yea, old notes like those
> Here are living on yet!—
> But of their fame and fashion
> How little these know
> Who strum without passion
> For pence in the snow!

Hardy hugged time to himself as he hugged pain and gloom; they were the three dimensions of his universe, in which he felt so much at home that he could be surprised when readers complained of its barrenness. It was thick and warm for him, like an old coat that exactly fitted him, even if it looked a little long, and indeed drooped to the ground. It was what he recognized as reality, the one thing to which he was entirely committed. The bitterness of the world did not forbid him to embrace it: a poor thing, but his own. At times, to be sure, he wondered whether he missed something that others saw; he peered hard, and had the reward of any pessimist—something was better than he expected. For that matter, many things were; even all things, if one did not mind their being just what they were. Now and then he would offer an apology for the low tones in which he spoke: he but sang his part, as others must sing theirs. There is in fact much kindness in him, a sort of subdued good nature which shines through his frown as well as his smile; for he smiled and was humorous, too, he had a nice sense of the absurd. He was susceptible to superstitions for which his philosophy would have had no use. Oxen *might* kneel on Christmas Eve; and of course there were all those ghosts; there was true love, too, a thing that mechanism would not explain.

His mind was complicated, and so was his art. The effect of plainness in his poems can make us overlook their skill: a conscious thing with him, and the product of study. He seems to be interested in nothing but accuracy of statement, even if this means that he must sometimes sound clumsy and crude; exactness is what he wants, and he will sacrifice everything to it. This is true; and it is true of any great poet; there is nothing else that causes us in the end to love poetry at all. But accuracy is itself an art, a fine and high one which all the muses conspire to praise. Hardy's muses, he said in 1887, were five in number: Form, Tune, Story, Dance, and Hymn. The last of these may surprise us a little until we read him through again and realize how often he was lyric in the rich, free, leaping way of the Elizabethans:

> This is the weather the cuckoo likes,
>   And so do I;
> When showers betumble the chestnut spikes,
>   And nestlings fly:

And the little brown nightingale bills his best,
And they sit outside at "The Travellers' Rest,"
And maids come forth sprig-muslin drest,
And citizens dream of the south and west,
    And so do I.

Or until we remember how various his stanzas are; he studied the stanza like a musician, and made it his idiom, whether intricate as in "The Discovery":

I wandered to a crude coast
    Like a ghost;
Upon the hills I saw fires—
    Funeral pyres
Seemingly—and heard breaking
Waves like distant cannonades that set the land shaking;

or simple as in "The Pine Planters (Marty South's Reverie)":

We work here together
    In blast and breeze;
He fills the earth in,
    I hold the trees.

He does not notice
    That what I do
Keeps me from moving
    And chills me through . . .

I have helped him so many,
    So many days,
But never win any
    Small word of praise!

Hardy was a musician; he was also an etcher. It was not for nothing that he had practiced architecture; the draughtsman in him is always coming out. He has the keen eye that feeling cannot confuse—an old man's eye, we are tempted to say, which misses nothing. Some of his poems are pure studies in black and white of things he saw in passing: "An East-End Curate," for example, or "No Buyers: A Street Scene," or "Nobody Comes." Others are masterpieces with weather for their theme: any kind of weather, for Hardy liked it all, but his specialty was rain, as in "A Sheep Fair":

> The day arrives of the autumn fair,
>   And torrents fall,
> Though sheep in throngs are gathered there,
>   Ten thousand all,
> Sodden, with hurdles round them reared:
> And, lot by lot, the pens are cleared,
> And the auctioneer wrings out his beard,
> And wipes his book, bedrenched and smeared,
> And rakes the rain from his face with the edge of his hand,
>   As torrents fall.
>
> The wool of the ewes is like a sponge
>   With the daylong rain:
> Jammed tight, to turn, or lie, or lunge,
>   They strive in vain.
> Their horns are soft as finger-nails,
> Their shepherds reek against the rails,
> The tied dogs soak with tucked-in tails,
> The buyers' hat-brims fill like pails,
> Which spill small cascades when they shift their stand
>   In the daylong rain.

Not that these particular sheep were before him as he wrote; a third stanza of the poem says it was long ago that he went to Pummery Fair, "and the hoarse auctioneer is dead." But time had not faded the impression—time, the sixth muse of Thomas Hardy.

The world of the *Collected Poems* is a great world. It is *the* great world, seen always as Hardy saw it, with quizzical, deep eyes that both formed and deformed it. But the deformation was no crime; it was rather a style, a way of twisting things into the shape his genius saw. This is often a queer shape. What other poet, wishing to tell his beloved that he would be hers even in the grave, ever expressed the hope

> That thy worm should be my worm, Love?

Worms were as much his specialty as weather.

> The leaf drops: earthworms draw it in
> At night-time noiselessly.

That is a small event among the many that take place in the great world. But Hardy noticed it, and having noticed it he must put it down. Of the several epitaphs he composed for himself, none is more simple and true than "Afterwards," with this refrain to be spoken by his neighbors:

> "He was a man who used to notice such things."

John Holmes

Surroundings
and
Illuminations

THE POET IS NOT POET OF HIM-
self alone, except in that last
hour when he writes his poem.
The poet writing, and the poet living his ordinary days, is ringed
about by powers and influences. Whether he is affected by them,
or with full awareness rejects them, the poet is a center of
surroundings and illuminations. From the outside it may seem
like Robert Frost's couplet, "We dance around in a ring and
suppose, But the Secret sits in the middle and knows." To
make possible more than supposing, and to remind the poet, who
is the Secret, I propose a metaphor of Stonehenge. There were
three of them. We know the ruins of mystery in the rings, and
the one thing we instinctively suppose is that there is a Secret
in the middle of it.

Four thousand years ago, herdsmen from the Continent made
Stonehenge I, a corral and butchering-place. The outermost
ring, three hundred feet in diameter, was a ditch eight feet deep,
its earth heaped in a bank at the inner edge, to keep cattle.
Stonehenge II was a temple built inside the ancient corrals, by

another population from across the Channel, two thousand years later. These people dug a ring of graves just inside the bank, filled it in time with cremated bones, bronze spear-tips from Ireland, amber beads from Europe, gold jewelry from Greece. The third wave of settlers set up two inner rings of pillarlike bluestone, brought with long toil from Wales by raft and roller. This was Stonehenge III, the one we know the ruins of. About 1500 B.C., sandstone slabs, shaped and brought from twenty miles away, were set up in a hundred-foot temple circle. Close inside them, the bluestone pillars from older rings were reset, and inside that a sandstone horseshoe around another of bluestone. The opening of the horseshoe, with certain guidestones, is toward the rising of the sun on Midsummer Day, June 24. At the center is a sixteen-foot block of sandstone, an altar; but in the metaphor I propose, that is where the poet sits, ringed round by more past than he knows.

I intend to make the Stonehenge metaphor work for me, not employ me. There are direct and meaningful likenesses. There are the recovered pillars out of the past, used again. There is the never-forgotten direction toward the sun. There are the barrows, layered with those objects that outlast man; tools; small, hard works of art; and bones of the body. And there is the evidence of incredible effort, generations of inexhaustible labor, and triumphs of constructive cunning. None of this was local. It was a time of translation, of interchange of skill and subject, a busy time of trading and exploiting. The archeological fact I like best is proof that the master planner and overseer of Stonehenge III was Greek. Someone knew how to bulge the huge pillars, and cut the lintel-stones wider at the top, for an optical illusion of straightness. Someone made mortise-and-tenon joints. Ten years ago, a carving on a Stonehenge column of a hilted dagger, of a type made only at Mycenae, only around 1550 B.C., was found, and made positive the presence far away and long ago of Greece in early England. One marvels and is reassured. It was the signature of an artist that outlasted. But my introductory image is not of antique and ruined stone. It is of an equivalent for the infinitely rich and available past, always nearer and always more available than we think, thanks to Celts and Greeks. There stand the rings, at any rate, of temple stones, of burial-holes, and earth walls against the wilderness, and in the center the Secret, the Poet. The surroundings I mean now are of active intelligence recording, evaluating, and discoursing upon poetry, and the illuminations I mean are of the perpetuators who love, and teach, and explain poetry.

It is with these that I shall deal, reminding more than informing, and by reminding, renew only once more, after all the renewals, the great inflowing and outreaching forces that prolong poetry's life. The poets are surrounded as they live and work, by presences of poets past and contemporary; by biographers; by reviewers and critics; by teachers; by editors and publishers; and by listeners and readers, that is, by audiences.

That there are wide waiting circles older than the oldest poet living, and as new as the newest first book, no poet is wholly aware. And he should not be very much aware; not when he is writing. If the poet looked up and around for approval, or veto, or help, it could turn into a nightmare of self-consciousness. He must balance an arrogant unawareness with a magnificent awareness, such a split personality as the actor knows, playing his part alone in a full theater. "One ruthless purpose, and that purpose poetry," is the secret the poet knows, sitting there in the middle of the ancient rings. Tradition, the monumental and hard-weathered past, is there to be used, stones as books to be rebuilt in the new temple. Stonehenge is his example even for building with old stone for new purpose; even when it is done in creative revolt; even in ignorance. Historical man is stronger than living man. The poet knows this, too. This is the Secret he finally cannot keep from himself, the ultimate mystery. My argument is that these other books, these companies and hosts at the ritual of writing the poem, do not interfere with, or become substitutes for, or in any way thin or distort, the poetry itself. Instead, they take up poetry's life and carry it outward, prolonging it in time, adding to it weight and worth it hardly had when it was new.

II

Some of those giant, silent figures standing out there in the dark are the poets, not stern and admonishing, and not benevolently nodding, either; but there. They are the poets our one poet has read. "Everything must ring like Elizabethan English," wrote Katherine Mansfield in a letter, "and like those gentlemen I always seem to be mentioning, 'the Poets.' There is a light upon them, especially upon the Elizabethans and our special set—Keats, Wordsworth, Coleridge, Shelley, De Quincey, and Co. Those are the people with whom I want to live, those are the men I feel are our brothers." For her they were, but for each poet they will be different. The best that the best of them ever wrote is the mark he tries for, despairingly or hopefully, and then at last with furious indifference. He knows that the least he can do is not shame himself in the eyes of Ben Jonson, who might laugh at him long and loud; or Rilke, who might not even hear him; or Thomas Hardy. How would one know if Thomas Hardy liked one's poem? There was a poet who found out. Charlotte Mew was given by his executor a British Museum Reading Room slip on which he had copied out one of her poems. She died two months later, in 1928, but reading Alida Munro's heartbreaking memoir, one rejoices that she did see that piece of paper. Mostly there is no such narrow margin, or no acknowledgment at all. We hear that Masefield admired Chaucer; that Frost read the Romans and Longfellow; and how many in our times have read and used Dante to powerful and relevant purpose, we know.

But this outer ring of giants is set there by the poet himself. No scholars guess the real influences from the poets to the poet. I can say that one of my giants is John Donne, who used a metaphor of power such as coins, mines, maps, royalty, and the sun, all symbolic of enormously concentrated authority. I like Herrick, but not Byron; Marvell and Campion, but not very much Browning; Blake, Milton, and Marlowe, but not Pope, Swinburne, or Spenser. Nearer the poet are a few poets of his own time. Winfield Townley Scott began so Robinsonian that it seems a miracle he escaped into his own language, one I envy and admire. Charles Olson seems not to have escaped Ezra Pound. Otherwise, how can I know the ring around Elizabeth Bishop, or John Berryman, or Vernon Watkins, poets of my time I much admire? They have their own secrets, as they are part of mine. Another poet whose manners, rhythm, and vocabulary are so pervasive as to stain the style of anyone who touches them is dangerous. Robinson is just such a poet, of course, and Pound, and so are Emily Dickinson, Hopkins, Eliot, and Frost. Who wants to be known as that young poet who writes like Emily Dickinson? I am wary in association with Robert Frost, and have consciously stood out away from his shadow and voice through thirty years of friendship. Like these others, he is one

of a kind. I have learned that from him. I owe more to the
Celtic wildness and superb formal control of Robert Graves
and William Butler Yeats. From Frost I learn management of
my life and image, and from hours and hours of talk, his talk,
I learn how living a restless mind at play can be. I like the dry,
wrenched understatement of John Crowe Ransom; the upper-
world infinity of Wallace Stevens, the exclamatory empathy of
William Carlos Williams, the delighted honor that Marianne
Moore pays to objects, the things of this world.

Among such figures, not influences in the textual sense, not
patterns in the imitative sense, is still another kind, what W. H.
Auden calls the Master. Auden said, in his Inaugural Lecture
at Oxford, in 1956,

> My first Master was Thomas Hardy, and I think I was very
> lucky in my choice. He was a good poet, perhaps a great one,
> but not *too* good. Much as I loved him, even I could see
> that his diction was often clumsy and forced and that a lot
> of his poems were plain bad. This gave me hope where a
> flawless poet might have made me despair. He was modern
> without being too modern. His world and sensibility were
> close enough to mine—curiously enough his face bore a striking
> resemblance to my father's—so that in imitating him, I was
> being led towards, not away from myself, but they were not
> so close as to obliterate my identity. If I looked through his
> spectacles, at least I was conscious of a certain eye-strain.
> Lastly, his metrical variety, his fondness for complicated stanza
> forms, were an invaluable training in the craft of making.
> I am thankful also that my first Master did not write in free
> verse or I might have been tempted to believe that free verse
> is easier to write than stricter forms, whereas I know it is
> infinitely more difficult.

So much for one of the rings. It has a much more personal
turn than I had expected from my rather ceremonial-sounding

metaphor of the Stonehenge circlings, but it is necessarily the one only the poet sees, the shadowy and shifting one, the listeners and watchers imagined by the poet at the center.

III

Henry James wrote a preface to Rupert Brooke's *Letters From America*, a young traveler's journalism. James, the conscious artist, said, "Nothing more generally or more recurrently solicits us, in the light of literature, I think, than the interest of our learning how the poet, the true poet, and above all the particular one with whom for the moment we may be concerned, has come into his estate, asserted and preserved his identity, worked out his question of sticking to that and to nothing else; and has so been able to reach us and touch us *as* a poet, in spite of the accidents and dangers that must have beset this course." Not many biographies of poets are concerned as wholly as Henry James would wish with the life-cycle of the poet's identity. The Rupert Brooke book was a fragment, a secondary document, as most biographies are. They answer more often the question, "Who was he?" than the question, "What was he?" Or if we learn what made him the poet who reaches and touches us as poet, it is because we know beforehand how the game came out. We can say to Keats, "Fool, can't you see you must not waste a year, for money, on a five-act play no one will ever put on? Begin the Odes now!" Reading Philip Horton's life of Hart Crane, we might wish to be on the boat homebound from Cuba, and tell the poet that having no new subsidized manuscript is no reason for jumping overboard. What a roll call of dolor, if every empty-handed foundationer committed honorable hara-kiri! Few poets live heroically to make brave biographies, or if they do, their poetry is probably second-rate. If Leon Edel has his way, and a new form and intention, the literary biography, comes into being, then we may have some monuments for my metaphor.

Yet I believe that poetry is the product of the whole man, not only not isolated from, but in every day nourished by his living. If we learn from the poets' biographies that, like everyone else, they have to do too much of what they have to do, the kind of biography Leon Edel and Henry James want would show us how this, too, made the poems. " The evidence is mulled over," Malcolm Cowley says, " all the details are fitted together until they begin to form a picture, vague and broken at first, then growing more distinct as the years pass by: the X or Y picture, the James Joyce, Paul Valéry, or T. S. Eliot picture. But it is not so much a picture when completed: it is rather a map or diagram which the apprentice will use in planning his own career." And John Crowe Ransom's poem, " Painted Head," while at one level it may be a treatise on portrait-painting, is another piece of evidence for the apprentices, in the poet's way of life:

> The body bears the head
> (So hardly one they terribly are two)
> Feeds and obeys and unto please what end?
> Not to the glory of tyrant head but to
>
> The increase of body. Beauty is of body.
> The flesh contouring shallowly on a head
> Is a rock-garden needing body's love
> And best bodiness . . .

In terms of biography, it says we understand the poetry the head made, the more we know about the life the body lived. Perhaps it is a little advanced for apprentices.

There is no poet's biography of our times to match William Butler Yeats's own life of himself. It was so constructed as to be one-third of his whole life-story, yet a book by itself, as the other two parts, his collected poems, and his collected essays, are books separately. Whichever is read first, the next is brightened by it, and the third by the first two. If a beginner could be advised, I would wish him to read the poems first, then the essays, which are black-and-white versions of the poems' color, and then *Reveries over Childhood and Youth*, and *The Trembling of the Veil*, completed later as *Autobiographies*. Perhaps no other poet's life ever or anywhere is as much worth reading. It is deliberately and magnificently and triply that assertion and preservation of identity that Henry James meant. To be sure, Ellmann, and Fraser, and Hone, and Jaffares tell us things about Yeats that Yeats does not. But when the figure is as great a figure of the artist as Yeats was, we read everything. We even procure the exhibition catalog, *Images of a Poet*, of paintings and photographs, printed books and manuscripts, shown in Manchester and Dublin in the summer of 1961. This is Ransom's rock-garden head and best bodiness indeed.

IV

Who says too much poetry is being written? It cannot really be the magazine editors and book publishers, because they gladly print ten times as much about poets and poetry as they print the poem itself. It would seem that they prefer the established fact, derivative from poetry, to that uncertain, not yet stabilized element, the poem—the new poem. In the terms of my metaphor, editors of magazines must seem the most monolithic of all the surroundings; barrier rather than benevolence. I think that the editorial function is doomed: an editor is a benevolent barrier. In the office of a major magazine other skills than the recognition of good poetry occupy editor's time and thought. A magazine staff is lucky to have one member willing to risk judgment of a poem. The poet's dealings will be with that one person, who will go elsewhere in two or three years. But the poet is lucky to find him, or her: this is one face of the real world.

It is different and far more to the poet's advantage in the literary quarterlies. Poets and critics of poetry read these, and book-publishers scout them. Their pages are the real arena where the important show is going on. The reward is prestige, attention, and reader-writer equivalence; not much cash passes. It is all rather otherworldly, but stimulating, responsive, much to be preferred. Editorial personalities dominate these magazines, and the best of them are warm and perceptive, and all poets come to know some of them. They are responsible to poetry itself, and if they are replaced, it will be by someone very similar.

The game of magazine appearances is so shifting and complex, so rivalrous and egoistic, and played on such a small field, it requires full-time watching with high-power binoculars. It's a good sport, if ego and energy hold out. Four hundred magazines print poems, but to achieve the right dozen for that important list of acknowledgments at the front of a first book, the utmost discretion, effort, and patience are necessary. Most people who write a poem think first of the *Atlantic Monthly* or the *New Yorker*, where the daily mailbags go out one door as fast as they come in another. Space for poetry in the big-circulation magazines steadily decreases, and even the littlest of the little magazines receives more than it can print. I think of poetry editors as distracted hostesses, greeting a totally unexpected guest while eyes flicker over already overcrowded rooms, and they make polite, meaningless remarks; that is to say, rejection slips. But now and then a good host takes charge, like the no-nonsense editor of the *New Orleans Poetry Journal*. Or a good hostess, like Harriet Monroe, who printed, I am sure, poems she did not like and could not really understand, in her magazine, *Poetry: A Magazine of Verse*, because she respected them. There are poetry editors like those, and will always be, I am sure. My metaphor ensures it.

Major book-publishers have a poetry quotient of two or three titles a year. They can afford to lose a little money on the chance of prizes, or for the sake of a balanced list. This is patronage publication, for which we may be as grateful as we may. Some of us turn into real publishers' properties, as they say; but problematical. We must never forget that the poet is not a businessman and that the publisher is not a poet, though both of them get mixed up about it. There are and always have been some brave book-publishers; among whom Alan Swallow of Denver stands high, for his long devotion to poetry. Some of the young houses seem more generously interested in poetry than the old ones. The finest poetry publishing venture in many years is being carried out by the Wesleyan University Press. But great things in poetry can be hoped for from some of the massive paperback publishers, if I read the signs right.

Nevertheless bewilderment is the typical look on the faces of publishers and editors as they stand round about the poets. In the general architectural scheme I describe, this ring stands rather sideways, stone face by stone face, the attention mostly somewhere else. The history of their own lists should prove to publishers that while one poet may be good for two to five books of poems, his future is good for ten or twenty books that will sell better. The complete poetry of Gerard Manley Hopkins makes a book less than one inch thick, but my incomplete shelf of books about Hopkins is two feet long. Yeats, whose own books are many, is stretched out to double his length. Rooms in libraries, whole libraries, are filled with books about Keats and Shakespeare; with decorative extra touches of original manuscript and statuary. The long-delayed complete poems of Emily Dickinson make three volumes; theories of her life are still coming out. I come to attention before the Robinson shelf. The line of his own published verses, narrative poems, and, alas, plays, is still much longer than all the books yet written about him as man and poet. An early appreciation by a Frenchman, Charles Cestre; a bibliography and a doctoral thesis or two; the life by Hermann Hagedorn; some letters, but nowhere near all there are—these, and Lawrance Thompson's inevitable selection, *Tilbury Town*, with its valuable preface, and Ellsworth Barnard's first-rate study of Robinson's total poetry, are little enough. But publishers will fill such lacks, being easier to convince on this than they were on Robinson's first poems. He paid for his own first book.

V

The good critics are the real responsibles in the temple of poetry I have schemed. To refer to the most ancient history of Stonehenge, critics must for their all-knowing purposes be in every one of the rings. They speak as if they had been, anyway. Surely critics were present when the first ditch was dug and the bank heaved up to contain the cattle; without any doubt they expressed an opinion of the original shape, extent, and digging techniques. Critics have long since rummaged in the burial-holes, and interpreted the beads and bones, the pot-fragments and weapon-parts. If in my metaphor the critics stand round the poet in an innermost ring, once upon a time they stood, and remember standing, in an older and outer ring. Critics remember and can judge the workmanship of every deep-based column, every mortised lintel; critics are quick to note a deviation from the master plan that was four thousand years in the carrying-out; critics always knew the temple's one purpose, which was to be ready for sunrise on Midsummer Day once every year. The critic is culture's conscience and memory and most severe in-structor, because his perspective is long and his authority abso-lute, being simply truth. His surrounding presence and his fierce illumination is first acknowledged and most feared of them all. To the poet the other ringing presences bring nourishment, furnishing, praise, or attention. The critic is judgment.

Critics make new concepts, because in their long perspective they can see relationships hitherto overlooked. Stanley Edgar Hyman nominates Kenneth Burke's *Attitudes Toward History* as the outstanding book in criticism, of the last thirty years, for giving us the concept of symbolic action. (Critics, I might say, do not by nature nominate one another's books for honors.) This is a concept in which literary forms are attitudes toward experi-ence. Literary works in the known forms become actions, for reader as well as writer. Despite the symbolic nature of these actions, they are as real and significant as any other. Therefore a poem is an action. Once this concept has been understood, it is never again possible to read poetry as one did before. Yeats, more by intuition and because he was a mythmaker, arrived at much the same thing. The poet who adds this tremendous faith to his stature need never doubt the poem's right to life. But more often what we get from the best critics is the closest possible reading of a text, with the fullest possible exploration of its sources and meanings. "To bring the poet back to life—the great, the perennial, task of criticism," says Eliot.

The ordinary reader of poetry, and I am an ordinary reader of it except that by avocation and devotion I have read more year in and year out than necessary, has first instinctive reactions to a poem; but does not trust them. Learning to trust one's first flashing reception is the secret. Reading Ezra Pound for the first time, I assumed that I was bewildered, ignorant, and mostly undesirable in Pound's audience. It was not that I did not experience the Cathay poems, or the *Draft of Thirty Cantos*, but I did not have, for instance, Kenneth Burke's assurance that a poem is an action for the reader. I did hear Pound's insistent voice in its many guises, but I could not tell myself that. I assumed I was bewildered. Not much later, I read R. P. Blackmur's "Masks of Ezra Pound," published in 1933 in *Hound and Horn*; I bought current issues of that unique and admirable quarterly. Blackmur said, with vigor and completeness and assurance, all that had dimly moved in my mind, all that I had not trusted in myself. These thirty years later, reading that essay again, it seems as right, as forthright, as final, as judgment can be.

In the same way, I look again with astonished and renewed self-trust at his early essays on Cummings' language; Marianne Moore's method; at his several essays on Yeats; again at the early and valid "Examples of Wallace Stevens"; and at his still continuing evaluations of Eliot. Blackmur seems to me the great critic of our time, our first best workman at the perennial task of bringing the poet back to life by reading him with fullest intelligence. The body of his writing, which includes much more reading and more difficult reading, of Henry James, D. H.

Lawrence, Melville, and others, would be paralyzing in its universal comprehension, if it were not that he writes so well, so like an impulsive, rational, brimming monologue by an expert. It demands the closest attention, but it can be read again, and will be read again. Blackmur speculates, too, and gives us reconsiderations and new conceptions, notably in his essay, " Language As Gesture "; his several essays on the art of criticism; and his important 1950 essay, " The Lion and the Honeycomb," which begins with the businesslike and infinitely promising sentence, " This paper proposes to examine into a certain section of the scholarship and criticism of poetry, and further proposes a possibility of expansion or growth for it."

What Blackmur does, we know is also done in exciting interaction by I. A. Richards, John Crowe Ransom, and T. S. Eliot; by principled independents like Louise Bogan, and Conrad Aiken, whose collected book reviews are basic reference; and by the best university essayists like Mark Van Doren, Cleanth Brooks, and Allen Tate—none of whom, in fact, would accept these categories. But all stand in those interwoven and everwatching rings in the new Stonehenge, where the poet imagines he is alone, but can never be alone.

VI

Crouched there on the sandstone altar, over his Stonehenge III portable typewriter, or yellow copy paper, the poet might seem a flash-lighted, peered-upon, public event, as important as a fire or car-wreck. He is not yet a public event, and he does not know he is being watched; he is lonely, wretchedly happy, he rages in words, he changes the world. But no one knows. Except that he shows the poem to his teacher in school the next day, and she knows the world is changed, or could be changed. Teachers do not know everything, but sometimes some of them know when they are seeing the world change. Sometimes the crouching poet has one of those teachers.

Because of this one or that one, in the seventh or the ninth grade, he gets on his feet. In high school, in college, it goes to his head, and luck or his chromosomes, or one of the other gods, crosses him with his last teacher. What is in his head is what will make him a poet, and the good teacher is the one who notices and makes living-room for the shape of his head.

But more teachers teach poetry than teach poets. Whatever our huddled bard was doing at his desk, if his name was Scott, or Longfellow, or Burns—or if it was Wystan Auden, Wallace Stevens, or Anne Ridler—teachers would make more of it to more readers than ever the poet most wildly dreamed. Some of them would do it wildly, and wash it down with emotion. Some dutifully, in the misery of drill, would chalk the standard metrical forms on the blackboard, and scan the lines of a poem. But more than any census can report, there are teachers who transmit poem and poetry. One knows they renew poetry year after year, because of a light that comes into faces of their former students as they speak of " the course they'll never forget." The name of the teacher may be famous, and more likely not, but the name does not matter; there are great teachers, faithful and expert and sworn, of both kinds. To see that lighted face at its best, a shining of gratitude, personal devotion, and lasting assurance, one may meet a former student of Mark Van Doren's. His extraordinary lectures on Don Quixote, in his recent book, *The Happy Critic*, or his paper on the poetry of Thomas Hardy, give others some idea of the delighted knowledge he imparts. And he produces teachers of poetry; there is no end to it.

I have in my head a landmark map of the colleges and universities of this country, each campus starred with the name of a poet who teaches poetry there. The universities are the real foundational patrons of poetry. They employ poets and cherish them and let them talk; the other foundations merely give away money. New England bounds and abounds with poets: Rolfe Humphries at Amherst, Richard Eberhart at Dartmouth, May Sarton and David Ferry at Wellesley, Richard Wilbur at Wesleyan; Peter Viereck at Smith and Samuel French Morse at Mount Holyoke; Robert Penn Warren at Yale and Robert Lowell at Boston University, or lately so; William Jay Smith at Williams; and round about the nation, John Logan at Notre Dame, Howard Nemerov at Bennington, Philip Booth at Syracuse, Elder Olson at Chicago, Randall Jarrell at North Carolina, Yvor Winters at Stanford, Theodore Roethke at Washington, Theodore Weiss at Bard, Helen Bevington at Duke, Richmond Lattimore at Bryn Mawr, Donald Hall at Michigan—it would make a rich address-book for a cross-country tour.

That any of them is academic, in the very worst sense of that word, or live in ivory towers, in the most ridiculous sense of that word, is flatly untrue. Each in his official life is probably the least academized, the least towered, member of the university faculty. The best thing about the literary-educational-social phenomenon of poet on the university faculty is that he is honored for being himself, a free-flying bird in a natural, worldly cage. It is the historians, the language professors, the chemists, who are caged, care-ridden, and committed nearly to death. The university poets are steady writers and frequent publishers, having the ideal situation for it. They teach either the writing, the history, or the evaluation of poetry, and thus exert prolonged and out-reaching influence. They review and discuss current poetry in the quarterlies, and in the largest newspapers and magazines. They are free to make public appearances, reading their poetry to audiences anywhere; to judge national poetry competitions; to help edit poetry magazines; and always and in the grand total, they are the hard core of the best audience for poetry. Professionalism, unquenchable appetite, or the juices of jealousy which in poets work very freely, make them the most ready and most constant readers of everything about poetry.

All these teachers of poetry, at every level, are better furnished with books and other materials than ever before. As textbooks, they have a range of anthologies, critical introductions to poetry as a subject, recordings by poets and other readers, and widely available magazine and newspaper material. The prime importance of poetry is assumed by the school and college systems, and abundantly supported by textbook publishers. Contemporary poetry has been taught by official consent and the teachers' knowledge for about thirty years now, which means that the beginnings were few and bold. But now there are several teacher-generations whose own school experience included modern poetry, and who know where to find it for classroom use—in paperback collections, in recordings, and so on. If the poet could see among his surroundings the ring of teachers, he might well feel crowded. But their direction is from him to students; they illuminate him not for his benefit but for the increase of his audience. He owes them more than gratitude. He owes them his life.

VII

One more ring, standing very close to the poet at work, might indeed jostle him, and seem to want to look over his shoulder while he writes, and to ask him to be a demonstrator of poetic composition, not one hard-breathing poet alone in a room with the English language. This watcher collects and studies the poet's very pages, the sheet after sheet on which he slowly forms his lines, and urges the poem into its right shape. This examiner of discarded work sheets re-enacts, as closely as he can, what the poet thought while he wrote—at the very instant, in the very setting down of the word. He cannot know all the poet thought and did not put on paper, but he can see in words written and crossed out, in lines roughly drafted and little by little smoothed and hardened, some tangible clues to what went on. He can reconstruct by intuitive guessing what the poet wanted to say, can feel the dulling and the firing of imagination. And he has the historical advantage over the poet of knowing beforehand how the poem did come out. He has his copy of the poem the way it now appears in books, the poem the poet hammered and scraped at in the rough, so doggedly making such difficult alterations that to the watcher seem so obviously, so easily, the changes that must be made. This new kind of scrutinizer, this doubleganger, this vicarious participator in the very pencil-work, is impelled to come as close as is physically and psychically possible to being the poet. Later he writes an account of the long step-by-step process he thinks the poet went through. The justification for this inside or almost-inside view is that nonwriters can learn from it how the poet's mind works. It is like taping electrodes to the skull, to listen to the brain's impulses. Either it is the most ruthless invasion of mind yet attempted, or it is the most daring exploration of the mysteries of literary creation. At very best—that is, even with much-scribbled-over work sheets for tangible evidence—it is an incomplete revelation. But this curiosity about the fits and starts, the rumblings and the lion's leap, that go on in the poet's mind, is a recent thing. I think the unspoken motive is an utterly innocent admiration for the unknown and unimaginable freedom of the poet's mind, a hunger for the supreme excitement of the artist's ultimate experience. I resent it, too. The poet's maunderings, wanderings, and fireworks in his subconscious and unconscious ought to be inviolable privacies. But the poet is doomed to ritual. When in my metaphor the sun rises on Midsummer Day, and the blazing light falls as the priests planned it, on the poet hunched there over his notebooks, the listeners and the watchers partake of the blood sacrifice. My metaphor is only a reminding device, though; the bleeding is not mortal. Poets like to bleed.

Reproductions of poets' work sheets have been appearing in textbooks on the understanding of poetry in recent years. Successive drafts are shown with as much realism as typography can manage—the cancellations, the alternate wordings, the unsuccessful early lines. Inch by inch a stanza grows, the poem grows, and we are allowed this close-up, this naked documentation. The supposition seems to be that if we share the struggle of evolvement, we more fully comprehend the poem. I am not convinced. I think it is like poking around a painter's studio when he is not there, and seeing what he mixes for his famous colors, how dirty he lets his brushes be, or what variety of sizes of brushes he has. Oil-painting is a messy and tedious thing, and a good analogy for writing poems; a poet's work sheets are tedious, and his workshop messy. The dominant and unsuspected fact is that so much drudgery went into the making. Such clumsiness, such mumbling—then the stroke!

One of the great collections of poets' notebooks and work sheets is at the University of Buffalo, in the Lockwood Library, made by the late Charles Abbott. Massive accumulators of rich raw materials know, I hope for his sake, that intention can be immortality. His intention was that poets and critics and teachers should penetrate the mystery of poetic composition. An exciting early result was Donald Stauffer's reactivation of R. P. Blackmur's poem, "Missa Vocis." In an essay called "Genesis, or the Poet As Maker," in a book Charles Abbott edited, called *Poets At Work*, Stauffer prints first the finished poem. He admires in much detail the apparently controlled total structure. Then he shows us six successive versions, in the poet's hand, and we learn after the most sensitive, informed, and obedient attention to the poem's growth, that " chance flowers into choice." We see that the way to write a poem is to write a poem. It begins cold and clumsy, warms itself, and marvelously, openly, to the astonishment of no one as much as the poet himself, comes alive in its own generative heat. Stauffer concludes that " the progress of the artist in creation is always toward greater purity, intensity, and unity," that the close examination of work sheets proves that it is the cumulative effect of small changes, of happy contrivings, of careful tending, that makes the poem the poem it meant to be.

Charles Abbott used to lecture on certain sets of work sheets in his collection. No one perhaps could or should follow the geologic growth of Dylan Thomas's " Hunchback In the Park," but the manuscript is available. It was a surprise to me that Kenneth Fearing tried out so many versions of an apparently effortless, colloquial New-York-talk piece. The Abbott collection shows almost endless testings of casual idiom, all trying to say the same thing, none quite right to Kenneth Fearing's ear. The reading and re-reading is tedious and very sobering, until at last the perfectly plain phrase comes. This tediousness was even more oppressive, and frustration greater, when Abbott presented

Stephen Spender's gropings for the now inevitable lines of "Landscape Near an Aerodrome." Spender's early notebooks are in the University of Buffalo collection. How could he write a run of such beautiful lines, and then so blindly not say what he must say next? Stephen Spender, of course, had not yet seen the famous poem in the anthologies of a decade later. But it is a shocking first lesson to beginning poets that their heroes have hands of clay more usually than the vision of gods, and that writing poetry is labor upon blind stubborn labor. There is a set of work sheets in this same library that shows Richard Wilbur's lively start at his poem, "The Juggler." Before the juggler begins to perform—and such airy performance at a country fair called eternity is the best of a Wilbur poem—the poet somehow came of several minds about the juggler's costume. He spent precious lines and energy on its checkerings, colors, till as the manuscript shows, he resorted to prose description of the simple event itself, before he could outlaw gravity, get the flashing balls into the air, and the poem going. The poem is a triumph, and it is a poem about triumph.

What these spyings show, as they occur in the inner precinct of the temple, where the poet works surrounded and illuminated by poets, biographies, editors, critics, teachers, and readers—these peerings and pokings—is how terribly poetry is cared for. I mean the uncontrollable curiosity, the powerful necessity of hunger and wonder about poetry, as beauty and terror draw us. These scrutinizers of the-poem-in-process are the really first readers; they read it before the poet reads it. They carry the report, plucked out of danger, back to the ordinary reader, to the teacher, further back to the critic and editor, and all the way back to the biographer. John Milton's ode, "At a Solemn Musick," has a line for which he chose the fifth of seven possibilities from his drafts. " To live and sing with him in *ever-endless, ever-glorious, uneclipsed, where day swells without night, in endless morne of light, in cloudless birth, in never parting light,*" became finally, " To live and sing with him in endless morn of light." Robert Frost wrote, " My little *mare* must think it queer," and " Between the *forest and the* lake," and improved both lines in revision.   Housman's alternatives are known, which would displease him; and Allen Tate's decade-long revision of his " Ode to the Confederate Dead " is a famous documented example in our time of the public claim and interest in such matters.   A wondering! but no wonder.

To review the concentric assembly I have summoned up in this metaphor of Stonehenge, in which all eyes fix the poet, is to confirm M. L. Rosenthal's idea that of all figures in 20th-century public life, the poet is the hero who can lead us to salvation. The poet seeks life with honor, for himself and us. Robinson recorded failures in the search; Pound recounts a bitter defeat and exile; Yeats more than any is the hero as poet, defies and despises politics and money-making, and magnificently completes his image of himself as artist; Stevens hides himself for art's sake, in art, the only salvation, satisfaction, and way of life. Our eyes are on the poet as hero.

May Sarton

This is the School of Babylon
And at its hands we learn
To walk into the furnaces
And whistle as we burn.

Thomas Blackburn

The School

of

Babylon

I MUST WARN YOU AT ONCE that I am not a critic, except of my own work, but perhaps I should not offer this fact as an apology for surely the great poet-critics of our time—Yeats, Valéry, Eliot—have used what has been sometimes taken as dispassionate criticism of others as a means of orienting themselves and of grounding their own work in an aesthetic. Perhaps criticism from poets is always self-criticism.

I should like to reconsider and shape once more some tentative answers to questions I have been asking myself for twenty-five years, questions about tension and equilibrium within the writing of poetry and within the poet's life. It is, in fact, just twenty-five years since my first book of poems appeared, and I am now close to the half-century myself, a good moment for such meditations.

Eugen Herrigel in a small but explosive book, *Zen in the Art of Archery*, speaks of the aim of the Zen masters as not "the ability of the sportsman, which can be controlled, more or less, by bodily exercises, but an ability whose origin is to be sought in spiritual exercises and whose aim consists in hitting a spiritual goal, so that fundamentally the marksman aims at himself and may even succeed in hitting himself." So let me draw my bow and point the arrow inward . . .

I have an idea that somewhere in his forties the poet reaches a turning point, at which he either becomes a more public or a more private person, that he has a choice, and on that choice depends the kind of work he will produce, as well as the kind of life he will live. In the dialogue between the world and himself, he fights to preserve the innocence and the intensity without which art cannot exist. And it is just when he is in his forties that the pressures to lecture, to review other men's books, and to be a public person begin to assert themselves. My theme is tension in equilibrium, that dangerous tension, that perilous equilibrium which exist in every great poem, and in the life of every poet; and I have just touched on one of the permanent tensions, that between the public and the private person, the poet who lectures and the poet who writes the poems: they are opposite poles. Each of us seeks out his own solution to this never-solved problem. Mine has been, in the last three years, to spend five months at least of every year in a village in New Hampshire. There I can study the ferocity of nature and realize (it is consoling in a way) that beside it the ferocity of poets and the critics of poets is child's play. But I suspect, nevertheless, that the tension between the public and private self is not an unfruitful one. One of the fascinations of Yeats' growth is that his assaults on the world, as a founder of the Abbey Theatre, and later as a senator, helped him to forge his style. Without the fierce tension between what he called "The Mask and the Self," would he have hammered out the iron of his later style? Who knows?

Tension . . . my Webster defines it in several ways. Here are three which I can appropriate: 1) A strained condition of relations, as between nations. 2) A device to produce a desired tension or pull, as in a loom. 3) *Elec.*: The quality in consequence of which an electric charge tends to discharge itself.

As I pondered these provocative definitions, I jotted down some of the tensions I experience in the process of writing a poem, tensions which discharge a load of experience in a most beneficent and exciting way when the piece of weaving on the loom turns out to be a real poem:

1) The tension between past and present,
2) between idea and image,
3) between music and meaning,
4) between particular and universal,
5) between creator and critic,
6) between silence and words.

Parallel with them are the tensions within daily life:

1) between the living and the dead,
2) between the public and the private person,
3) between art and life.

Once I had noted down these apparently organized but actually haphazard ideas, I took refuge at once in the equilibrium and organization of a poem, Thomas Blackburn's "The School of Babylon," from which I have borrowed the title of this essay. (The relief it was to rest in this "momentary stay against confusion"!) I might tell you that the epigraph of Blackburn's poem is from Daniel, "Men loose walking in the midst of fire" (3:25). This is the second and final stanza:

Although a wine-glass or a cup
Can hold as little of the sea
As you and I of our own selves,
Pin-pointed by mortality,
We still, that something of the whole,
May quicken in the finite part,
Must labour for a deeper breath
And greater tension of the heart.
Out of their windy distances
The further energies draw near
And kindling in our tongues and hands
Increase the glory and the fear.
But still as the unspoken word
Swings slowly downward into speech
And in becoming us reveals
Another word beyond our reach,
We praise the School of Babylon,
For where else could we learn
To walk into the furnaces
And whistle as we burn?

Of course, one of the springs of poetry is our strained relations
with our own immediate past, the warring nations within the
self; then the poem itself becomes a device by means of which
this electric charge discharges itself. And one of the springs of
poetry is joy—joy and grief as opposed to happiness and depres-
sion; the difference in in*tens*ity between the former and the
latter is my point. In a formal sense, each poem also discharges
and balances the tension between the whole past of poetic
invention and itself; each new poem is partly propelled by the
formal energies of all the poems that have preceded it in the
history of literature. Those poets who wish to affirm their
freedom from the past by pretending that all old forms are dead,
deny themselves this fruitful tension. Their poems are intended

to be wholly " present," but we experience the present as a kind
of equilibrium between past and future, and there is only tension, no balance between present and future. Such poems, like
the children of *Brave New World*, are test-tube poems. I think
that the answer may be in the distance in time between the
points of tension: we have to move back more than one generation to find the fruitful polarity. Valéry makes this clear in his
unexpected praise of Victor Hugo (the poet's Hugo as against
the public's Hugo) for going back to the then unfashionable
sixteenth-century French poets for some of his forms. So Hugo
remains a source in a way that Vigny, de Musset, Lamartine
do not.

" The poetic player," as Valéry puts it in another context,
" can choose his game: some prefer roulette, others chess." If
you are a chess player, what you are looking for is a new opening,
a new device by which you may win within the old rules; a
means of taking your opponent by surprise. The dynamics of
form have to do with our initimate relation with the past, and
our natural instinct for what we can use for a particular poem,
the form that can best become a vehicle for its electric current,
the tension between the whole rich past and this poem *now*.
Like a pregnant woman who must suddenly have strawberries,
I once found myself going back to Herbert for the form of a
poem which created an equilibrium for me (in this case a
permanent one) out of the excruciating tensions set up by my
mother's death from cancer. The poem itself I could only write
four years later; I could write it partly because I had found
in George Herbert a viable structure.

Sometimes the polarity expresses itself, not through metrics,
but by means of an echo. Eliot has often used this device, in
the earlier poems for purposes of irony, in the later ones as a

way of condensing time. How effective it can be, Yeats proved
in "A Bronze Head," when suddenly he allows Herbert and
the particular reverberations Herbert brings with him to act as
catharsis for his revaluation of Maud Gonne. I need not remind
you of the climax of Herbert's "The Collar":

> But as I rav'd and grew more fierce and wilde
> > At every word,
> Me thought I heard one calling, *Child*!
> And I reply'd, *My Lord*.

Here is the third stanza of "A Bronze Head":

> But even at the starting-post, all sleek and new,
> I saw the wildness in her and I thought
> A vision of terror that it must live through
> Had shattered her soul. Propinquity had brought
> Imagination to that pitch where it casts out
> All that is not itself: I had grown wild
> And wandered murmuring everywhere, 'My child, my child!'

And let us not forget that, as Valéry says, "Everyone knows
that to aim at not following or imitating someone is still in some
way to imitate him. The mirror reverses images." The poet
cannot escape from the tension between past and present even
when the tension is expressed by total rejection of the past.

He cannot do so any more than any one of us can escape
from our own individual past, for to do so is to murder a part
of ourselves. The tension between the living and the dead,
especially perhaps that between oneself and one's parents, after
their death, may become especially powerful in middle age.

John Holmes and Richard Eberhart have been overtly concerned in their poetry with finding and explaining the equilibrium between themselves and their parents. (Again we pull

the bow far back to loose the arrow). Eberhart can say it all
in three lines:

> And I stare, rich with gifts, alone,
>
> Feeling from the sea those terrene presences,
> My father's hands, my mother's eyes.

Yeats' father and grandfather are always there back of the poems,
and so too with Edwin Muir. I must regard my whole life as
an attempt to bring into focus and so be able fully to use the
rich gifts I was given by a scholar father and an artist mother,
each strong in his own right. I do not summon them, but they
are there, pivotal tensions. Everything must be tested and questioned against their innocence, their passion, and my whole life
a precarious balance between their two kinds of genius.

   Let us return to poetry itself and the writing of poems. At
once I find myself rebelling against the act of criticism because
it must, if it is to explain anything at all, make an indivisible
act divisible and partial. In fact, it is possible that we recognize
the birth of a true poem as distinct from what Louise Bogan calls
"imitation poems" by this very state, a state in which a series
of complexes exist *together*, and find their way to equilibrium
without ever having been separated out into distinct functions
or threads. Idea and image, music and meaning, creation and
criticism, the particular and the universal, silence and utterance—
when we are ready to write a poem, all these separate modes
work together at the same time. "Poetry," as Valéry puts it,
"must extend over the whole being; it stimulates the muscular
organization by its rhythms, it frees or unleashes the verbal
faculties, ennobling their whole action, it regulates our depths,
for poetry aims to arouse or reproduce the unity and harmony
of the living person, an extraordinary unity that shows itself

when a man is possessed by an intense feeling that leaves none of his powers disengaged." Unfortunately the act of criticism imposes the necessity to disengage certain powers, and is therefore always in some sense, false.

A true poem does not begin with a feeling, however compelling, and of course we feel a great many things that never become poems. A poem emerges when a tension that *has been* something experienced, felt, seen, suddenly *releases* a kind of anxious stirring about of words and images; at this moment there is a mysterious shift of energy; the energy that was absorbed in experience itself, now becomes an energy of an entirely different kind, and all that matters is to solve the sort of puzzle, the sort of maze in which certain phrases, and a certain rhythm lie around like counters in a game of Scrabble. So a great grief may turn into a certain kind of imaginative energy and lift the sufferer right out of himself into the joys of creation.

Let me give you a ludicrous example which will serve as well as any to give you some idea as to how the process works. Some years ago, shortly after I moved into my New Hampshire house, I was given a magnificent Teddy bear as a Valentine and he has become one of the Lares, sits on a big desk in the little parlor and emits a muted bellow when you pick him up. One day I seemed to hear him singing a little song, a rhyme, and, once in my head, I could not get it out for a whole day. It goes

> Only, only,
> lonely, lonely,
> moanly, moanly,
> groanly, groanly.

True poems may make their appearance in just the way this rhyme did, and take over the day, interrupt whatever we may be doing, insist on making themselves heard, willy-nilly. For us, who are not Teddy bears, the music may be more subtle, though it may not (you remember Edith Sitwell's "Daisy and Lily, lazy and silly," no doubt?). In a true poem, this "musical stir" as Maritain calls it, this tension of a phrase asking to be musically resolved, is always accompanied by an image. The rhyme of the bear is not a poem for many reasons, and one is that the bear himself does not appear. If the bear-song could have incorporated bear himself, it might have become one. Everything in the psyche takes place for a reason. Why did something in me identify itself with the Teddy bear? No doubt I too was feeling lonely and moanly. If this state had been about to be translated into a poem, I would have had to enter the maze of bear, the puzzle of bear and find my way out of it, or rather *into* its center and heart. And I might have sat down to ask myself some questions.

Did the bear begin to sing for me because he suggests innocence, childhood, and also the whole unconscious animal world, the sensual world, of which at that time I felt deprived? And is the sensual world always there when we feel wholly ourselves? So that to be deprived of our animal self is in some way to be deprived also of its polarity, the angel self? The bear seems also to be consolation—he sings a lonely song because I feel lonely, and I am comforted by this image of childhood. Why is an image of childhood consoling to an adult?

But while I am asking myself these questions, the music the bear is chanting runs along all the time underneath, emerging now and then into an actual phrase, imposing upon me the metrical form the poem will take. And a high tension, a delightful inner humming is set up between the apparently innocuous rhyme, the image back of it, and my own response, both conscious and unconscious, to what is going on in my head.

There are points at which the arts, especially those of painting and poetry, bisect each other. Painters, too, think their way through, by means of images lifted out by a present shock of emotion, and polarizing the whole past. I want to steal here a fairly long excerpt from Ben Shahn's book *The Shape of Content.* He is analyzing the sources of a painting of his called "Allegory." The immediate seminal image was that of a fire in Chicago in which a colored man had lost his four children.

It seemed to me that the implications of this event transcended the immediate story; there was a universality about man's dread of fire, and his sufferings from fire. There was a universality in the pity which such disaster invokes. Even racial injustice, which had played its part in this event, had its overtones . . .
I now began to devise symbols of an almost abstract nature, to work in terms of such symbols. Then I rejected that approach too. For in the abstracting of an idea one may lose the very intimate humanity of it, and this deep and common tragedy was above all things human. I returned then to the small family contacts, to the familiar experiences of all of us, to the furniture, the clothes, the look of ordinary people, and on that level made my bid for universality and for the compassion that I hoped and believed the narrative would arouse.
Of all the symbols which I had begun or sought to develop, I retained only one in my illustrations—a highly formalized wreath of flames with which I crowned the plain shape of the house which had burned. . . .
The narrative of the fire had roused in me a chain of personal memories. There were two great fires in my own childhood, one only colorful, the other disastrous and unforgettable. Of the first, I remember only that the little Russian village in which my grandfather lived burned, and I was there. I remember the excitement, the flames breaking out everywhere, the lines of men passing buckets to and from the river which

ran through the town, the mad-woman who had escaped from someone's house during the confusion, and whose face I saw, dead-white in all the reflected color.

The other fire left its mark upon me and all my family, and left its scars on my father's hands and face, for he had clambered up a drain-pipe and taken each of my brothers and sisters and me out of the house one by one, burning himself painfully in the process. Meanwhile our house and all our belongings were consumed, and my parents stricken beyond their power to recover.

Among my discarded symbols pertaining to the Hickman story there were a number of heads and bodies of beasts, besides several Harpies, Furies, and other symbolic semi-classical shapes and figures. Of one of these, a lion-like head, but still not a lion, I made many drawings, each drawing approaching more nearly some inner figure of primitive terror which I was seeking to capture. I was beginning to become most familiar with this beast-head. It was, you might say, under control. . . .

When at last I turned the lion-like beast into a painting, I felt able to imbue it with everything that I had ever felt about a fire. I incorporated the highly formalized flames from the Hickman story as a wreath about its head, and under its body I placed the four child figures which, to me, hold the sense of all the helpless and innocent.

The image that I sought to create was not one of *a* disaster; that somehow does not interest me. I wanted instead to create the emotional tone that surrounds disaster; you might call it inner disaster.

When I read these pages, I recognized the analogy with a poet's images and how he unearths them. For here, too, we may sometimes begin with an actual scene, witnessed, but it will only become material for poetry if it is able to magnetize to itself a part of the inner world as well, if it reverberates. There is some truth, I think, in the criticism of the poets called "academic" (I fear I am one of them!) for being overconcerned with the decorative aspects of language. A poem does not move us deeply, I believe, unless the central image is capable of stirring us below the level of consciousness, is, in fact, an archetype. For the metaphor holds the explosive power of the poem. This explosion may take place on the surface of the mind, in which case it gives a moment's pleasure, or it may take place in the mysterious inner recesses of being, in which case the poem may well do what Rilke asks of art at the end of his sonnet on the "Archaic Torso of Apollo":

> Here there is nothing that does not see you:
> You must change your life.

The most viable metaphor contains the greatest possible number of tensions and at the same time releases them. And we are changed by it not because we have been told about something, but because a whole series of inner actions have been set in motion by it and at the same time to some extent resolved. Something has been changed at the center of consciousness, forever.

The surface image is a temptation to every poet; for if he is a poet at all, he is apt to think in images and every abstract idea comes to him immediately translated into a concrete exemplar. But every time he writes a real poem, he will find himself polarized in a tension so complex and painful that it forces him to deepen and explore below the surface. It is the complex charge of the image in Richard Wilbur's "The Grave" that gives this poem its power . . . at first a private dream, the return in dream of the dog he had loved as a boy and did not have the courage to bury when it died; this image explodes by the end of the poem. Through it, Wilbur is able to make a cool deep incision into all our guilt about the dead, and to let some of the poison out. The poem in this instance is an act of grace.

Tension between idea and image has to do with the depth and complexity of the image; if it is an inspired image, i. e., one that comes from deep enough below the surface, it may very probably change the original idea, for the image is all the time pointing the way to what we really mean, and not what we thought we meant. In this sense the image is ethical. As Bachelard, the French psychologist who has devoted himself to examining metaphor, says: " we are here at a center where ideas dream and where images think."

" The Combat " by Edwin Muir throws us a naked metaphor so powerful that I have never recovered from my first reading of it, and to re-read it is merely to resume aloud, the uninterrupted reverberations that it set up.

> It was not meant for human eyes,
> That combat on the shabby patch
> Of clods and trampled turf that lies
> Somewhere beneath the sodden skies
> For eye of toad or adder to catch.
>
> And having seen it I accuse
> The crested animal in his pride,
> Arrayed in all the royal hues
> Which hide the claws he well can use
> To tear the heart out of the side.
>
> Body of leopard, eagle's head
> And whetted beak, and lion's mane,
> And frost-grey hedge of feathers spread
> Behind—he seemed of all things bred.
> I shall not see his like again.

As for his enemy, there came in
A soft round beast as brown as clay;
All rent and patched his wretched skin;
A battered bag he might have been,
Some old used thing to throw away.

Yet he awaited face to face
The furious beast and the swift attack.
Soon over and done. That was no place
Or time for chivalry or for grace.
The fury had him on his back.

And two small paws like hands flew out
To right and left as the trees stood by.
One would have said beyond a doubt
This was the very end of the bout,
But that the creature would not die.

For ere the death-stroke he was gone,
Writhed, whirled, huddled into his den,
Safe somehow there. The fight was done,
And he had lost who had all but won.
But oh his deadly fury then.

A while the place lay blank, forlorn,
Drowsing as in relief from pain.
The cricket chirped, the grating thorn
Stirred, and a little sound was born.
The champions took their posts again.

And all began. The stealthy paw
Slashed out and in. Could nothing save
These rags and tatters from the claw?
Nothing. And yet I never saw
A beast so helpless and so brave.

And now, while the trees stand watching, still
The unequal battle rages there.

> The killing beast that cannot kill
> Swells and swells in his fury till
> You'd almost think it was despair.

There, I hope you will agree, is an image in poetry that can be set beside Ben Shahn's lion-head of fire.

Just as we "must labour for a deeper breath and greater tension of the heart" when we come to use or discard the metaphors that pass through the waking mind when a poem is in process, so we must labour too, to deepen, and even sometimes roughen, the too facile music that floats about on the surface of consciousness. Yeats spent a lifetime working toward the tone, the rhythm, the tune that would express the rigor and complexity of what he had to say as he moved away from the superficial singing of the Lake Isle toward the resinous speech of the Last Poems. In a letter of 1916, he is already worrying this problem: "I separate the rhythmical and the abstract. They are brothers, but one is Abel and one is Cain. In poetry they are not confused for we know that poetry is rhythm, but in music-hall verses we find an abstract cadence, which is vulgar because it is apart from imitation. This cadence is a mechanism, it never suggests a voice shaken with joy or sorrow as poetical rhythm does. It is but the noise of a machine and not the coming and going of the breath."

Poetry finds its perilous equilibrium somewhere between music and speech, and each poet as he comes along has to breathe his own breath, find his own intervals that will make it "sound right" for him. How various the solutions may be can be apprehended if we juxtapose Robert Frost and Paul Valéry! One reason I have found myself going back to Herbert is to try to catch his intervals, the swing of his pendulum between music and meaning, between music and speech . . . we are not floated

down the poem like paper boats; we are absorbed into it by
strange little pauses and irregularities of breathing, as if indeed
a voice were speaking aloud to us now:

> Ah, my deare angrie Lord,
> Since thou dost love, yet strike;
> Cast down, yet help afford;
> Sure I will do the like.
>
> I will complain, yet praise;
> I will bewail, approve:
> And all my soure-sweet dayes
> I will lament, and love.

Even when he uses this simplest of all forms, you see, the
cadence is highly individual, his own voice.

Once again—it is, after all, my theme—what becomes clear is
that facility (lack of tension) is the enemy of poetry. The very
poverty of rhyme in the English language gives us an advantage,
I sometimes think, over the French poet, crowded in, as by a
flock of pigeons, by the hundreds of rhyming words. Rhyme in
English is a hard master. The obstacles that it raises in the
current of our thought slow us down, make us think, and of
course also sometimes (there is a saving grace!) bring us the
lucky chance that may enrich meaning in unexpected ways.

> I could give all to Time except—except
> What I myself have held.

says Mr. Frost. Might one not speak in somewhat the same
terms of the struggle within the writing of each poem? A great
deal has to be given up, so that when we come to the end, we
do say, "And what I would not part with, I have kept." We
have come through some real dangers and taken some real risks.
The music, the images, and the propulsive idea, all these make

intricate and sometimes apparently opposite demands. From the tensions between them, when they arrive at an equilibrium, poised on all the dangers, like a bird in the air, the poem soars. As Henry Adams says at the end of *Mont St. Michel and Chartres*, "The equilibrium is visibly delicate beyond the line of safety; danger lurks in every stone."

I fear I have been rather solemn about what the French troubadours knew as the "gai scavoir." But I hope it goes without saying that, just as the joy of playing tennis for the player is the mastery of the continual stress of the game, and if it were easier to play, it would not be half as much fun, so the poet of course is never happier, nor more wholly himself, than when he is engaged in the play of writing a poem, in making the puzzle "come out right." And the longer he can tease it along, the happier he is, if he is a poet like Valéry. Of course there is the final danger of crossing the intangible frontier beyond which a poem is damaged by more manipulation . . . it may suddenly go dead like the mouse which the cat has played with. When is a poem finished?

The answer is, I think, when all the tensions it has posited are perfectly equilibrated, when the change of a single syllable would so affect the structure that the poem would fall like a house of cards under the shift. But Valéry's answer to when a poem is finished would be, "never." Valéry was that rarest of poets—one for whom the ultimate release was in the artifice itself (he did not *want* to finish), as against Yeats for whom the release was in equilibrating tensions *back* of the poem *by means* of it. Yeats could say, "They and their sort alone earn contemplation, for it is only when the intellect has wrought the whole of life to drama, to crisis, that we may live for contemplation and yet keep our intensity." Valéry could say, "My poem 'Le Cimetière

Marin' began in me by a rhythm, that of a French line . . . of ten syllables, divided into four and six. I had as yet no idea with which to fill this form. Gradually a few hovering words settled in it, little by little determining the subject . . ." I need not remind you, I am sure, that this turned into one of the few great metaphysical poems written in our time. It is clear that we do not exactly choose our poems; our poems choose us.

Poems may never be finished if one is Valéry, but essays must come to an end. It was my intention when I began to think about *The School of Babylon* to avoid using any poem of my own as illustration. But it now seems to me that the analysis of someone else's poem, one of those by John Holmes, Richard Eberhart, Richard Wilbur or Randall Jarrell which would have been appropriate, could be an act of hubris. For who am I to describe the process by which any of them came into being? I can only speak with authority about process in relation to my own work.

Probably Thomas Blackburn's poem moves me as it does because it articulates almost every element that goes into the writing of poetry and the poet's life as I see them. The refrain of the first stanza, the one I did not quote goes:

> This is the School of Babylon
> And at its hands we learn
> To walk into the furnaces
> And whistle as we burn.

Here we find Yeats' vision and Valéry's fused. We must be "men loose walking in the midst of fire," and men or women who find it possible to whistle as they burn. The writing of poetry is the whistling. But if we did not dare walk into the furnaces, there would be no occasion for whistling. Whistling in the dark is another matter!

We go to school to a complex, demanding art so that we may learn a device for discharging tensions and apprehensions which we might not otherwise have strength to bear, and which as it is, become simply transposable *energy*. So grief itself is transposed into a curious joy.

I shall close with a poem of mine called "Lifting Stone." The image came to me through a painting by Katharine Sturgis, a semiabstract water color of a piece of granite being lifted out of a quarry. I saw the painting first more than ten years ago, but could not afford to buy it. Still, it haunted me. And when it reappeared, in a show, still unsold, years after my first meeting with it, I felt this was a sign. I had better buy it and live with it and understand *why* I was haunted.

The image was evidently one of those complex ones which had something to reveal if I could explore it down deep enough, explore it by making a poem out of it. Quarries give us to dream. I sensed slowly that one of the reasons why is the fact that we dig down deep into the earth to bring up the stones that will eventually soar in the cathedrals—as we dig down to the subconscious matrix to bring up the images that fertilize the imagination. No height without depth.

But there was another element in the painting, the equilibrium of the pulley itself, lifting this immense stone pillar on a steel thread, as if the stone were a mere feather. Here tension could be seen equilibrated in the most delicate possible way. Thirdly, in Katharine Sturgis' painting, the whole composition centered in the abstract figure of a man, standing way down deep inside, directing the operation. I had at the time, been reading Herrigel. Let us go back to him for a moment now. Herrigel worked for five years with a Zen master in Japan before he even began to learn the self-abstraction and the technical

skill to understand the art of the archer. Sometime in the fifth
year he tells us,

> One day the Master cried out the moment my shot was
> loosed: "It is there! Bow down to the goal!" Later, when I
> glanced towards the target—unfortunately I couldn't help my-
> self—I saw that the arrow had only grazed the edge. "That
> was a right shot," said the Master decisively, "and so it must
> begin. But enough for today, otherwise you will take special
> pains with the next shot, and spoil the good beginning." . . .
> During those weeks and months I passed through the
> hardest schooling of my life, and though the discipline was
> not always easy for me to accept, I gradually came to see how
> much I was indebted to it. It destroyed the last traces of any
> preoccupation with myself and the fluctuations of my mood.
> "Do you now understand," the Master asked me one day after
> a particularly good shot, "what I mean by 'It shoots,' 'It
> hits'?"
> "I'm afraid I don't understand anything more at all," I
> answered," even the simplest things have got into a muddle.
> Is it 'I' who draws the bow, or is it the bow that draws me
> into the state of highest tension? Do 'I' hit the goal, or does
> the goal hit me? Is 'It' spiritual when seen with the eyes of
> the body, and corporeal when seen by the eyes of the spirit—
> or both or neither? Bow, arrow, goal and ego, all melt into one
> another, so that I can no longer separate them. And even the
> need to separate has gone. For as soon as I take the bow and
> shoot, everything becomes clear and straightforward and
> ridiculously simple . . ."
> "Now at last," the Master broke in, "the bowstring has
> cut right through you."

What held me here, as it did in Katharine Sturgis' painting
was once more that at the point of highest tension, lies also
the point of supreme release. In the end what is most difficult
becomes most easy, what was heaviest to lift becomes light as

air . . . and this happens, of course, when we are not thinking
of ourselves at all, but have become instruments of an art or
craft. At such a time it may be possible for a master like Frost
in the art of poetry to sit down after a long night's work on
something else and set down "Stopping by Woods on a Snowy
Evening," without a pause, as a Japanese painter in one stroke
paints a piece of bamboo and it is "right."

Lifting Stone

This is an ancient scene: we stand and stare
As hills are excavated and then lifted;
Swung on the cable's perpendicular,
The load is pivotal to earth and air,
A feather-balance, and so delicate
The stone floats up as if it had no weight.

Below, a solitary figure stands
To gentle the long bundle from its bed;
Athens and Troy are leaning from his hands;
The Roman arch, then perilous Chartres ascends
Out of the empty spacious world where he
Nudges rich burdens toward history.

Who with his own machineries of skill
Has not dreamed often of this very place?
Painter and poet lift the buried hill
To build a pyramid or clean bright wall,
And the great spires that sleep in this quarry
Are excavated toward the clouds they marry.

What soars is always buried deep for ages,
Gently explored in the hill's dark mind,
Prized, hewn in slow thoughtful stages,
Then floated on these airy equipages,
Watched by a figure standing there alone
Whose work, humble and hard, is lifting stone.

Richard Eberhart

Will and
Psyche
in Poetry

I WISH TO EXAMINE THE RELA-
tion of Will and Psyche to poetry.

I conceive these terms as op-
posite poles of a modern dichotomy, but they may lie at the
root of the mind itself and go back to the beginning of thought.
I choose them because they have impinged upon my consciousness for years. It would be possible to attempt a reduction of
the reality of poetry under a multiple aegis, or to accept a uni-
tarian principle. However, it is natural to me to think in terms
of dualism; if it is too neat to cast everything into either black
or white, it is also orderly, and forces an arbitrary, though not
conclusive, order on what is discovered.

The presumption of poetic criticism is intellectual authority.
By thinking about poetry one can make certain determinations.
This is the play of the mind, a pleasurable exercise. I do not
say that truth is to be found, nor that what authority one comes
by is not itself subject to the sway of time. What I affirm is
the relativity of truth within absolute limits and the normalcy
of a dichotomous look at poetry. There is a certain modesty

in my approach. One does not wish absolutism, but a relative sagacity. After reading criticism for thirty years, it is necessary to wipe the slate clean, and speak freely with all one's impurities upon one. There is a vast body of historical poetry, to which accretions are always being made. It may be of interest to look at certain types of poetry, certain poems under an arbitrary canon. I shall study poetry from the creative, or poet's, point of view rather than from the presumptions of a reader who is not a poet and has no desire to write poetry. Maybe the line between creative reading and creative writing is thin. Maybe the approach of a dualism here is mythical. In any case, my remarks shall be, I hope, exploratory rather than dogmatic.

In thinking of Will and Psyche a battery of descriptive terms comes at once to mind. Will is of the body; Psyche, or Soul, is of or beyond the mind. Will is flesh; Psyche spirit: Will is active; Psyche passive. Will makes something happen, or wishes to make something happen; Psyche makes nothing happen. Will is impure; Psyche is pure. Will represents struggle and effort; Psyche represents an uncontaminated grace. Will is the body of this world; Psyche is the elusive, passive, imaginative quality of or toward another. Will is interested; Psyche is disinterested. Will goes back to some basic power in the cell, an animal exercise. The cell has an excess of energy over its power to maintain itself.

Psyche is at once mysterious and eludes the simplest opposition to what I have just said. I suppose it depends upon a cellular structure for none of us living can feel what it is to be dead and only by imagination, by intuitive leaps, can we dream beyond death. Here many ideas about Psyche appear. If one equates it with soul, then we may say it is the soul; but nobody knows what the soul is. I have touched my flesh for years trying to find my soul. I have still not seen it. But there are ancient, persistent ideas about the soul. There is, for instance, the Platonic world soul, envisaged as a vast amorphous cloud hanging in the heavens. When we are born a portion of the world soul is attached to our body, where it lives while we live; when we die, it ascends, or departs, depicted in old paintings always upwards, back to the mother lode or static whole of the world soul. There are all the variations of Eastern philosophy, thought, and religion about the soul and the afterlife. However, to write the last few sentences I must be corporeal; it is easy to insist upon this! Therefore, by reason we may say that we do not know whether we have a soul, but without an undue amount of sympathetic projection we may assume that we have a soul, a Psyche, somewhere about us.

In a short space and time the easy absolutes mentioned above have broken open into what may be seen at once to verge upon massive speculations. This is part of the fascination of the problem. We start by saying that Will and Psyche enforce a real dichotomy, but almost at once it is seen that these terms exfoliate and proliferate; that there may, maybe must, be some Psyche in Will, for how could it be so base a thrust as by strong nature not to possess some qualities of the divine? And how could Psyche be so pure as not to possess some qualities of base human nature? They may not be white and black as we suppose. Indeed, it may be that some of the greatest poetry lies between them, partaking of both, giving the critic a complex pleasure of discovery and evaluation. It may be, depending upon the nature of the critic's piercing look, that Will poetry and Psyche poetry represent only a small part of the whole, to be enjoined by special pleading, but loved when found. I admit this as a possibility.

Of the two components in our dichotomy, Psyche appears to be more elusive, to ramify into the more interesting complexities, to be the harder to grasp since its pleasing quality resides in its ungraspable part, and by the notion of some kind of grace, whereby the mind does not wish to probe, nor the intellect to meddle, but the whole being to accept, when in the grip of Psyche poetry, thus immediately ceasing to be a critic. But enjoyment may be had either way; there are as many ways of enjoying poetry as there are ways of living. And I do not say that Psyche poetry is better than Will poetry. I say that it is more subtle, more elusive, more delicate, essentially I suspect more overwhelming by its virtue to take us in against our will, leave us suspended in delicious realms of ambiguity, unresolved conjurations, passive pleasure. It works partially through a religious attitude.

I have a short poem which appeared in *Reading the Spirit* in 1937 but which was written I think while I was at Cambridge, between 1927 and 1929. It was written to the world at large, to nobody in particular, and was entitled *The Critic*. I wish to turn this poem upon myself. It goes as follows:

> The Critic with his pained eye
> Cannot my source espy
> For truly and purely to eye it
> He would have as critic to die.
>
> I with joyful vision see,
> I cannot his purpose acquire.
> For if the Critic were truly free
> He would love, and not be a liar.

It may be interesting to quote first a poem which is neither purely of Will nor of Psyche, but which contains admixtures of both. I no doubt thought of myself both as poet and critic. I was under the eye of I. A. Richards, and was aware of his early belief that all that modern poetry can do is to make pseudo statements, in fact, tell lies. His psychological point of departure was that in the modern world the scientist alone demonstrates truth; this is the truth of putting one thing to another and calling it, logically enough, two. This is the truth of physical experiment where, given certain facts, certain results must follow. There is rigidity and absolutism. William James enounced this reasonable world in his essay on pragmatism. A thing was good if it worked, which was analogous to the one-to-one conclusions of the experimental scientists. Americans allowed only what worked and now we were becoming great. The assumption was that this was good.

Let us see what my short poem said. It posited in the first line a pained eye for the critic. This is an arbitrary choice of a word, meaningful and setting the mood when quickly followed by the notion that the pained eye of the critic cannot espy or find out the source from which the poet writes. It sets up a dichotomy between poetry and criticism; one is supposed immediately to sympathize with the poet and believe what he says is true. The first stanza ends on the extended notion that the critic would have to die in order to see the source of the poet, or see into it.

The second stanza begins by saying that the poet sees with joyful vision; the assumption is, simply, that the critic does not. In the swiftness of the poem this is supposed to be taken un-challenged. But it is not, of course, necessarily true. The critic is not directly attacked, but the emphasis is placed on the differ-ence of the poet, who cannot " his purpose acquire." Here is a difference, upon contemplation of the poem, that may not at first appear. The critic, in stanza one, might achieve the source

of the poet were he to die as critic. The poem does not specify
the methods for this dying, nor indeed state what kind of dying
it is, psychological or imaginative. But in line two of the second
stanza the poet, because he sees with joyful vision, cannot acquire
the purpose of the critic. This is, in fact, dogmatic assertion
and pleads specially for the poet. It seems to understand instinctively that creation is first and criticism second and that this
is the natural and just order of things. The poem may in fact
be hostile to criticism because of the latter's power, recognized,
but not stated, to be injurious, even deadly to the creation of
poetry. It may therefore arbitrarily assume that the critic has
no joyful vision, which in cold reason nobody would allow, while
the poet has a superior hold on ultimate value. The last two
lines cap off or clinch the central idea of the poem. They say
that if the critic were truly free he would love, and not be a liar.
What gives the poem its life is the terseness and economy of the
expression. Words like "truly" and "purely" are placed, in-
stantaneously, to work efficiently, without the mind having to
stop to ponder them. At the end there is a tacit boon extended
to the critic; in fact, the antilegislation of the first quatrain is
taken back in the "if" proposition which assumes that maybe
the critic can be regenerated. It is not to say that he cannot.
If then in fact he were truly free, he would love, and not be a
liar. The word "love" at the end runs back to the beginning
and ties in the idea of love as intimate to the act of creation,
in poetry here, as well as in fact in nature. Close association
is made between love with its joyful poetic vision and truth.
If the critic were truly free he would not be divorced from the
nature of poetry and he would not have to tell lies about it,
which is his professional business, but by loving he would tell
the truth.

The immediate tone of the poem impresses the obvious dichotomy upon the sensibility; but with reflection and in reading it carefully, it will be seen to be a rather hopeful poem. This ultimately hopeful quality is the Psyche part of the poem, while its thrust and somewhat belligerent immediacy is its Will part. There is the elusive notion that there is something sacrosanct in the source of the poet, which is we may say his Psyche; and, still turning it around, if the critic will exercise Will he may find through love the truth. It seems to me to be neither a true poem of Will nor of Psyche, but to live and persuade with elements of both.

II

Before going into old definitions of Will and Psyche, let me propose two short poems which exemplify some of their characteristics. There is a famous four-line poem, supposed to be sixteenth-century, which many know, an anonymous piece entitled " The Lover in Winter Plaineth for the Spring." It is a poem of the Will.

> O Western wind, when wilt thou blow
> That the small rain down can rain?
> Christ, that my love were in my arms
> And I in my bed again!

This is simple, direct, evocative, a cry from the heart. It is a poem of wish fulfillment as good now as when it was written. It has a positive, strong emotional force. In the death of winter, loveless, the poet longs for spring, which represents love. The ejaculative utterance of the last two lines is powerful. Physical love is celebrated as an absolute good. There is no doubt about

it. Calling upon Christ is a brilliant thrust. The renouncer of
the world is called upon to bring the world most closely home
to the heart. Although exceedingly short, this is a whole poem
written in the fullness of humanity, with ardent belief in life
and in love. It is a direct poem of the Will.

A poem which comes to mind when thinking of Psyche is
Poe's "To Helen," wherein Psyche is named. This is a good
example of Psyche poetry in a pure, or almost pure form. There
is practically no Will in it. If we tend to equate Will poetry
with Romanticism and Psyche poetry with Classicism, this poem
in its form, its balance, and poise, is classical. Poe's emendation
of his lines in the second stanza, to come on "To the glory that
was Greece / And the grandeur that was Rome" is a famous
example of improvement by taking thought. If these words
were written as a prose phrase they would not seem remarkable;
they might pass as journalism. Set as they are, with three major
g's neatly muted by five minor r's, they become memorable.

The poem reads as follows:

To Helen

Helen, thy beauty is to me
　　Like those Nicean barks of yore,
That gently, o'er a perfumed sea,
　　The weary, way-worn wanderer bore
　　To his own native shore.

On desperate seas long wont to roam,
　　Thy hyacinth hair, thy classic face,
Thy Naiad airs have brought me home
　　To the glory that was Greece
And the grandeur that was Rome.

Lo! in yon brilliant window-niche
　　How statue-like I see thee stand,

> The agate lamp within thy hand!
> Ah! Psyche, from the regions which
> Are Holy Land!

Where you feel in our anonymous lover of the sixteenth century his loss of the loved object, and are in no doubt about the strength of his conviction that it would be good to have his love in his arms again, in bed, the reader feels no such strong pull toward its object in this poem. It is a much subtler, finer matter entirely. The poem ends in a sigh, a sort of wistfulness, a recognition that Psyche is so far removed from ordinary affairs that one can only dream about her from afar, not clasp her. She is way off in the improbable distance where her capture would be the remotest possibility. The notion of Psyche as soul is thus intrinsically honored by the poet. This a magical poem, an object of contemplation, having little to do with action.

For all its famed simplicity the poem has a good many ambiguities and subtleties. We are supposed to think of Helen of Troy at once, yet some readers, primitively blessed, may think only of some other Helen. I read this poem for years without knowing what a "Nicean bark" was, and have again by this time forgotten, but this ignorance does not destroy the poem. The main sense is clear. The phrase "weary way-worn wanderer" always struck me as effeminate in the nineteenth-century sense, Swinburnian or late Tennysonian; I have never seen the most fatigued sailor who would fit this description. A plural number is suggested because of the plurality of barks. If they were actually weary and way-worn they would stop wandering, quit, give up, and go home. This is a romantic notion of an improbable kind of sailor, to put you in a mood of dream. We have encountered the notions of gentleness and perfume already. The barks and the men have actually got home, due to the persuasion of the beauty of Helen, which draws or pulls slowly but inevitably as a tide.

In the second stanza " desperate " is a well-chosen oppositional word and is the only one in the poem that suggests violence of action. The reader has to put up with certain nineteenth-century locutions in the poem, such as " barks of yore," " o'er " as elided, and " wont to roam." These are easily taken in. The first line of the second stanza, " On desperate seas long wont to roam," mounts an ambiguity which is probably not recognized at once by the reader; Helen may be thought to have roamed long on desperate seas as the prize of the Trojan wars, or it may be the poet-reader-adventurer who has done this, the Ulysses spirit. A suspension of meanings involves us in a smooth syllabic flow while we do not have to entertain its underlying mechanisms.

It is obvious that if Poe had transposed " glory " and " grandeur," the poem would not be great. If he had said the " grandeur that was Greece," which would have after all have been possible, " and the glory that was Rome," he would have made a political mistake. The word " glory " has been used for Rome, just as we have our " Glorious Fourth," yet it is elementary that Poe, and probably a lesser poet than Poe would have done the same, perceived " glory " as specially pertaining to Greece, " grandeur " as specially pertaining to Rome. The homing notion of the first stanza is reiterated in a different way. The " hyacinth hair," " classic face," and " Naiad airs " are here the home-bringers, not now just to a native shore, but to the magnitude of spiritual and worldly dynasties.

In the first stanza we do not see Helen, it is not a photograph. It is an intellectual idea. In the third stanza we have a masterful placement, a dichotomy one part of which is a standard conception of a statue in a window-niche, an art object with a certain plastic reality to it, holding aloft an agate lamp, while almost at once this is contraverted by Helen turning into Psyche, "from the regions which / Are Holy Land." There is a great deal of magic cleverly dealt here. First, Helen-Psyche is only "like" a statue, she is "statue-like," so we are in the midst of poetry as a reality shot through with simultaneously-held possibilities. Second, we are invited into a never-never land which takes us unawares, as it were, in the last two lines. They are so finely woven, as is the entire piece, that we accept at once, without the necessity for analysis. The words of the last stanza enforce, in a subtle, gentle way, a mood. The whole poem breathes a mood of gentleness and opens on far contemplations.

For instance, "Lo!," an antique word which we take in stride, is followed by "in yon brilliant window-niche." We do not have to notice the "yon" much, but it is as if a finger were pointing to an actual place, yet poetic vagueness is subsumed, we see no real building; we do not have indication of the architecture if Poe had any in mind; we do not know the material size nor the shape of the window-niche. Poe as magician casually uses the word "brilliant," but this has intellectual implications with regard to the lamp and the meaning of Psyche's light.

"Ah! Psyche" involves us in the ultimate tone of the poem. Psyche, or soul, is from regions which are holy land. The sighing tone of this realization has in it tenderness and longing, yet there is no hint that this sacrosanct reality may be dealt with outright. That is the beauty of the poem. It is Psyche poetry, beyond the will of man. An ultimate reality is addressed. This reality, the soul, is admitted and placed in a true position beyond action. It is a matter almost of religious devotion, at least of religious affinity. Note that in stanza one there was a home coming, in stanza two that there was a further type of home coming, and I had meant to mention the ambiguity of "brought me home," which may refer back to the weary mariners or exist merely as a cant phrase, whereas in the last stanza, as if to progress to the highest spiritual plane of contemplation, there is no action at all, only a serene, ultimate sight to be seen and contemplated, beyond possession, and beyond use. "Holy Land" obviously may refer to the Holy Land and I suppose this sense is to some extent in most readers, intellectually inviting us to impose Jerusalem upon Greece and Rome. One wonders whether Poe intended this. I do not think so. The stress is on "regions." I think as magician-poet he is using valid poetic means, where words taken in usual connotation have overtones of other connotations which may be brought into focus in the mind, or left as a vaguely-felt pleasure. He is having his cake and eating it too to use "holy land" here as the very end of the poem.

The main thing to say about this satisfying poem is that there is a holy land but that we may not get to it. We may contemplate Helen but we may not touch her. If it were a Will poem there could be some anguish because of this fact. Because it is a Psyche poem there is no anguish; the poet is beyond this and the reader is beyond it too. Psyche is the region beyond strife and as Helen it is mythical and fabulous. A light is held on the world. We may contemplate this beauty, which is ultimately impersonal, spiritual, and ineffable.

Sometimes one mumbles certain phrases or lines of a poem in a sort of somnambulistic rite. Sometimes one does this for years. Many poems in English are great because of only a line or a phrase, or a few lines. Almost every school boy has learned "Helen, thy beauty is to me" and if as a man this phrase alone should persist as more memorable than another, it would perhaps be because of his will to violate the poem and possess Helen! If you say "Helen, thy beauty is to me" and stop there you have paid a debt to Poe as poet and as anarchic individualist you have thought to do the impossible, to possess Psyche itself. With that we leave Poe, Helen, and Psyche to the ages. They all age beautifully.

Let me now tell the traditional story of Psyche. It is interesting that the concept of Will has exercised the minds of great thinkers to a great extent and that there is a vast amount of lore on the subject. It is equally interesting, and instructive for our own definitions and distinctions, that encyclopedic notions of Psyche are limited in scope, that there is no vast amount of lore, and that the meanings tend by the nature of the subject to be cast into story, fable, or allegory.

The tale of Cupid and Psyche, in the *Metamorphoses* of Apuleius, is interesting as the only ancient fairy tale which is told as such. In it Psyche, the youngest daughter of a king, arouses the jealousy of Venus, who orders Cupid to inspire her with love for the most despicable of men. "Cupid," continues the *Encyclopaedia Britannica*,

however, falls in love with her and carries her off to a secluded spot, where he visits her by night, unseen and unrecognized by her. Persuaded by her sisters that her companion is a hideous monster, and forgetful of his warning, she lights a lamp to look upon him while he is asleep; in her ecstasy at his beauty she lets fall a drop of burning oil upon the face of Cupid, who awakes and disappears. Wandering over the earth in search of him, Psyche falls into the hands of Venus, who forces her to undertake the most difficult of tasks. The last and most dangerous of these is to fetch from the world below the box containing the ointment of beauty. She secures the box, but on the way back opens it and is stupified by the vapour. She is only restored to her senses by Cupid at whose entreaty Jupiter makes her immortal and bestows her in marriage upon her lover.

The Greeks were lucky in living on two planes at once as if there were no contradiction, no dichotomy. They lived in the reality of the earth and in the reality of the heavens. Thus, they were able to invent a pantheon of gods and talk about them as if they were quite like themselves, yet giving them simultaneously the devotions of a different species. Psyche stands for the soul, is a term for the soul, and it is not strange that the Greeks should have told of Psyche in terms of a love story. So the soul and love are intimately allied. And this soul and this love are not so far from immediate concerns as not to have, in the story, all manner of worldly and painful trials, commissions of error, whims of fate; yet the fact remains that the story has a happy ending. The last sentences of the story, as charmingly told by Edith Hamilton (*Mythology*, p. 100) read "So all came to a most happy end. Love and the Soul (for that is what Psyche means) had sought and, after sore trials, found each other; and that union could never be broken." If we say also that poetry is love we have a *raison d'être* for the great amount of Psyche poetry there is in literature. And sometimes, in a plausible moment of illumination, we see things in a clear, fresh way as if for the first time and know that a fairy story with a happy ending is equal to any other interpretation of the world, acceptable as real. Then the obscurity and burden of our minds settles down into our perpetual modern cynical or doubting consciousness.

The fundamental distinction in all the ratiocination of the philosophers about Will is the primary one that it is always stewing in its own juice, is always hoist with its own petard,

is always there in the meshes of the flesh, a bestial or an intellectual thing; whereas the primary qualities of Psyche are harmony, reconciliation, beauty, peace, a timeless at-oneness with
some ultimate value, a fairy story with a happy ending which
is possible only because the idea of Psyche is the most elusive,
the most delicate, the most ephemeral and thus, paradoxically,
the strongest and most complete repository of mortal awareness.
Psyche becomes a myth just as does the Virgin in Christianity.
She is love, as the story was told above, and the fairytale maker
had the penetration to see that his lightness of touch really
embraced and went beyond all the ponderous effects of the
willing animal man. It is possible to take a fairy tale with the
deepest seriousness, it is so wonderful and playful and ultimately
meaningful. But in our time we do not often do so. We think
of ourselves as too realistic.

In our short Will poem about the lover who imprecates
Christ to bring his love to his arms again, we are not concerned
with any part of Psyche. It is physical love that he wants, a total
involvement of flesh and manhood. There is nothing against
this, it is itself a kind of noble charm. But it presupposes that
the lover will be completely joined to him in the kind of love
union he wishes. But in the Psyche story love goes beyond itself
to an airy and ethereal truth, subtle and deep. There is the
suggestion of the danger of looking too deeply into nature in the
lamp-light vigil of Psyche over Cupid. The burning oil is a
sort of fatal flaw which makes the loved object disappear. But
Cupid represents forgiveness at the end of the story and we
note that Psyche is made immortal by a god. This is all beyond
the proper realm of reason. It is unreasonable. It pays implicit
homage to the idea of mystery in human affairs, just as it is true
that in marriage one never knows one's mate and that an elusive

reality is an essence of marriage although it may be practiced for twenty or forty years. With this background, let us return to Will and, while holding judgment in abeyance, throw out some notions of what it is.

There is something about Will which is eternally youthful. The Will, progressing through the flesh with time, a gift of life in its deepest resources of power, has in it all that is wild, free, eager, joyful, the giver and taker of dangers, superior to, while being enmeshed in, all sorts of evils. Will is fresh and lean. Will works beneath the intellect while seeming not to and drives the personality to new action. Will is behind all aggressiveness, all savage deportment. It is there in the subduing of forests, the erecting of cities, the building of armies, acts of war. It gives off death as quickly as it shows forth enlightenment. Brain power is sometimes largely will power. Will is a torment of abuse and the search for perfection. It is a gift of nature. Its symbol could be the impassioned rider spurring the horse. It can dream of universal brotherhood but also of atomic destruction. Cunning, craft, malice, intellect; aspiration, desire, plan, thrust, perseverance, control; faculty, persuasion, peculiarity—these are all willful and are absolutes dominated by the blood-drench, the flow in the veins, the strong life sense, the urgency to dominate, the pleasure of action, the health of a death-violating eye, freedom, and joy.

Freedom and joy! How little freedom and joy there is in the world. They must be made anew, forged in an active principle of blood, in a causative art. This necessity was recognized by Blake, Hopkins, and Lawrence. It is Will that will create the world anew; Will that will make something happen; Will that will make happen the compulsive poems. This also Whitman knew. The Will poet writes with the whole personality in a full thrust; he is totally engaged in the strength of his realization. A dynamic urgency burns in him; he is alive with vitality, love and aspiration and malice and scorn. I think of Crane writing *The Bridge*.

Now we come to a major problem of poetry. Does it conduce to action? Does it exert a cause from which there must be an effect? Is it offensive, distasteful, and does it make one wince? Does it fire one to perhaps even patriotic action? Who would nowadays think of Longfellow as a revolutionary poet? Yet was not " Paul Revere's Ride " a revolutionary poem and did not Americans respond to his " The Ship of State? " Would not the latter make them ready to die for their country, that is, long ago? Yeats at one point wanted his poems to spur Irishmen to militant action.

The Will conduces to the action of the poet in writing the poem. All poems attempt to persuade in some way. We now arrive at the problem of communication. And we may as well go back to our anonymous sixteenth-century short poem of the poet calling for his love to be in his arms again. I should say that this sort of successful short poem creates an immediate state of identification in the reader. The reader has no difficulty in placing himself in the position of the poet so that he too is bereft of his lover and with equal passion wishes for the fulfillment cried out for. The poem is universally valid for the majority of mankind. The reader thus identifies himself with the material of the poem. It has made something happen in that it has made the reader feel exactly as the poet felt. We have to add that the full sway of this poem does not necessarily bring on the desired result. There is something comical about a despairing lover. The poem does not say that the desired result is achieved. It is instead a strong wish-fulfillment; but

I suppose we could hold, without loss of dignity, that if the poet willed strongly enough he would actually find a solution to his difficulties. The poetry has made love happen. Love is the purity of his concern. The problem seems fairly clear in so simple an example. On the other hand, in a Psyche poem like Poe's "To Helen" we have ultimate ambiguity and fluidity, as if the poem lived in a perpetual continuum of unresolved possibilities, whose best communicability is its tempting, fascinating, and endless ability not to give up its secret, not perfectly to communicate, but to float in a magical dew and timeless sight of something seen but not touched, imagined but not possessed, aspired to but not achieved, so that the residue of feeling from this poem is like the feelings about the soul itself. It is a poetic mechanism for preponderating the soul.

III

Let us retrace our steps. The problem of Will and Psyche was announced as a dichotomy, but had hardly so been stipulated than the neatness of this dichotomy was seen to have blurred edges. A search through literature may discover pure poems of Will, as defined, and pure poems of Psyche, as defined, yet the definitions may not be exhaustive and there is a peril that any poem adduced may not be as pure as it seems. The Western Wind poem, about the immediacy of the desired for love, physical love, seems purely of the Will; indeed, it may be quibbling not to think it so. And yet there is the speculation, as one of a problematical number of final connotations, in this case few, that a reservation should be supplied to the intention of the poem; the mind can conceive that it does not go far enough, for nothing is said about the nature or quality or meaning of the love that is cried for in the lover's arms and in bed. We are supposed to blind ourselves to any raveling out of thought. The success of the poem primarily keeps us within bounds; its strong, willful force binds it into a self-contained breathing machine. Except for the critic. The critic may play with these four lines, ranging over them discursive claims. What if the positive thrust of the poem have negative, even disastrous results? There is much love that brings on grief, endless trouble, every form of madness, even suicide, and may give rise to tragic literature. Only a critic would think that there is a lack in the poem because some ultimate result of the predicament is not specified or intimated. Could as great, or as enduring, a poem have been composed, which would also be of the will, if the old Elizabethan had cried out, let us say, in an excess of the kind of manliness that found its exercise and reward in seafaring, new world discovery, or hand-to-hand combat:

> Christ, that my love were never in my arms
> And I in my bed again!

I doubt if the poem would have lasted so long. Yet in the actual poem there is a frustration in the writer which makes it come into being: in my emendation there would also be a frustration, only a different kind of frustration, a modern one. If he were in his bed without his lover, wanting none, but wishing the spring and the rain, he might have recourse to extensive dreams, he might in fact be a performer in the realm of Psyche poetry.

But this gives a comic touch and may perhaps show the limits of criticism. It is not, in a sense, fair to go so far. It is uncalled for. It is not reasonable. Criticism must be based on logic and reason, on scope and judgment. The poem would seem therefore to suggest its own circumference for discussion. If one goes beyond that circle, one is committing bad taste. Bad taste must be excess beyond the facts, that is, sentimentality, and it must be fundamentally wrong-headed. I have produced the above out-of-focus locution to attempt to show that criticism ought to stick to the main course, to look directly at the words and sensible connotations of a poem, not to go off into brainful asides which destroy the cogency and neatness of the suggested poetical system. But I also give it as a warning that the difficulties of criticism are many, and extreme, and that poetry is an unruly horse not easily ridden with elegance.

We then had an example of so-called pure Psyche poetry. Poe's "To Helen" has a restraint, an elegance, a fairness of proportion, which does not invite destruction by easy opposition to make it a willful thing. It stands as an example of enduring, mood-producing, elusive poetry, and the only comment I have finally to make on it in the context of our subject, is that, however tender and wistful and suggestive its ultimate feeling may be, Poe yet had the will to write it. So the problem is still there. If he had only day-dreamed the poem, not composed it by strict, calculating, and masterful art, we should be the losers by his lack of will.

It is possible to think simply and clearly. Perhaps the great thinkers have done so. It is also possible, and just as human, to think unclearly and in a profusion of confusions, jumping this way and that, going off on tangents, trying to grasp meanings out of the air, so to speak, and great thinkers have done this. Life is complex; a famous apology for complexity in modern poetry is that it is so because modern life is complex. There is a sort of tenacity in the mind to resist conclusion. To conclude is to arrive beyond Will at stasis and finality. It is the Romantic point that to strive is better than to arrive; the struggle toward definition is more rewarding than whatever may be gained from final conclusion. Hell is more interesting than heaven; evil more provocative than good. But I suppose it depends upon the age, the age's characteristics. The eighteenth century provided a static society, a well-ordered and neat outlook on life; thus came didacticism in Pope and Dryden. The nineteenth century brought on the hidden beast in the machine, so we had the rumblings and exalted strikes-through of Romantic, assertive individualism. The twentieth century brought to flower in its first half a monstrous bloom of societal chaos, so we have a great poem like " The Waste Land " in a nonassertive revolution of intentions which penetrated into the surrounding chaos itself and brought forth chaotic resolutions.

What is a Psyche state in poetry? I would wish to continue without definition, dwelling in an ambience of vagueness, willfully shirking the duty of defining heaven. I would like to have my Psychic cake and eat it too, and not tell what it is made of! I would like to advance the cause of subtlety, mystery, and the ineffable. However, one cannot talk to no purpose, thinking runs to conclusion, and it is a pleasure to don the mantle of a sometime critic, from which I state, simply, that a Psyche state in poetry pertains to, exemplifies, or takes off from peace, quiet, calm, security, harmony, proportion, concord, tranquillity, freedom as from something (war, for instance), serenity, stillness and silence. Now to give Will its same and simple due. Will is wish, desire, inclination, pleasure, appetite, passion, purpose, determination, choice, intention, entreaty, command, decree, power, arbitrary disposal, self-control as in a man of strong will, zeal, volition.

I wish to be clearly understood in this paper that my dichotomy is arbitrary, existing as a framework for the discussion of works of poetry fitted more or less arbitrarily into my scheme because of my love of the poems chosen. I make no claim as a philosopher to any new original concept about Will and am in fact in awe of all the heavy ratiocination about this term in the history of philosophy. Likewise of Psyche I do not write a new story of Psyche to equal the Greek. On both of these terms I have levied my own definitions, but I like to resist conclusions because there can be no real conclusion to literary criticism. It is a living, breathing, continuing thing.

Then also I want to make it clear, at the risk of repeating, that literary criticism is not a science, cannot be accurate in the way that a physical experiment may be accurate, and has its pleasures in a humane attitude to what is at hand. Ambiguity is one of the charms of modern poetical criticism. I entered these delighting reaches early. While I was at Cambridge, my classmate William Empson was writing, as a man in his early twenties, that seminal book *Seven Types of Ambiguity*. I want to conclude, very shortly, with an anecdote of what happened to a Roman poet who wrote an ambiguous line under Caius Caligula.

But we have to deal with literary criticism. Therefore it seems sensible in this paper to give you some added notions about it. Of the types of poetical criticism the evaluative is best. It represents a lofty attitude. When practiced by a judicious, not a prejudiced mind, the results may be salutary. When practiced by prejudiced minds, the criticism is thrown down into the arena of politics. Politics is the low view, moiled in human error. Political criticism has little or low value. It does not aim at the truth, nor at justice, but at chance, distraction, and temporality. This is not to say that political criticism should be outlawed. We must suffer it along with the greatest. It is part of the stability of democracy to entertain it. But the intention is impure.

The intention of evaluative criticism, in a judicious mind, is high. It strives to seek the truth about a work of art and to communicate this truth to the reader. All manner of subtleties of perceptions are available to this type of criticism. It does not rule out a-priori scaffolding, which accounts in part for Dr. Johnson; nor does it rule out elusive intellectual concretions, which specifies, sometimes, Coleridge. It does not say that the New Criticism necessarily has the last word in any ramifying arguments, neither does it allow that the neo-Aristoteleans have the last word. Evaluative criticism in an honest and perceptive mind seeks to establish life-giving relationships within the art and between art and society. It neither wishes to overpraise nor to underrate. It may propose unwitting prejudices in the very structure of mind, in that mind is always idiosyncratic; the reader allows for this and in reading Empson, for instance, much of the fun is in acceptance of his peculiarities of temperament which give on to the liveliness of his sometimes far-fetched presentations. Yet few would say that, totally speaking, he was not devoted to finding out the truth about a literary work. It takes some wit to appreciate wit.

I have no objection to categorical criticism, and assume we have yet to see a totally categorical criticism mastering the entire aesthetic intentions of the West; the field is so vast and wide none has yet had the arbitrary ability to contain it. Dante in his *Commedia* wrote the best criticism of the medieval time, but in a sense it seems too easy: his world was unified. Goethe had a harder task and did less well. Eliot in our time leaned upon modern Christianity and seemed to take in not the whole, but parts. His view has the feel of the limited. It beguiled us for decades but, as Mr. Blackmur perceptively remarked, we tend to read "Four Quartets" instead of the Bible. We get the Bible through modern religious poetry. There is something very wrong about this. Dante's work was so happily integrated with the total religious integration of his times that one has no feeling of this sort of substitution when reading the *Commedia*. Perhaps this was a lucky and happy fall of historical events, that is all.

It may be that the *aperçu*, the unschematized, personal intuition is as good a type as any, maybe better than most, in our present state of taste. Students tend to rebel, for instance, at Yeats' hard-won schematization in "A Vision" which, although fascinating, fails to satisfy due to arbitrariness and straining. Few really love it. Many can admire its conic elaborations but it somehow does not take in all of life. They give it admiration, along with understanding, but they do not give it love, which it does not invite. It may be that the relatively few, somewhat undisciplined, but thoroughly human asides, chance perceptions, and penetrating remarks by Frost represent the best criticism about poetry, a criticism not of a school, also not eccentric, but wise flashes of truth thrown off easily, if sparingly, down the decades. Too much criticism is a noose around the neck of creation. Each reader should be his own critic, should be strong to hold in abeyance final judgment on any criticism, lest he lose his soul. I propose abeyance criticism. It points up enjoyment, tones down tomb-cold finalities. Let us keep the doors of perception open.

Now we know the bold outlines of our dichotomy and we see that much pleasure of poetry resides in ambiguity, that Will and Psyche conjoin to destroy any simple black-and-white approach to them, and we will find, perhaps, a great difficulty in ever getting beyond the idea that ambiguity is a prime source of pleasure in the art of poetry; that vagueness and irresolution are values leading to possibilities of prolonged enjoyment; and that nothing ultimate about poetry can be scientifically clear.

Yet in ancient Rome a poet lost his life because of ambiguity. It is in a somewhat facetious mood that I conclude by presenting the Emperor Caius Caligula as critic, absolute and mad. This wild man lived twenty-nine years (A.D. 12-41) but fortunately ruled only three years, ten months and eight days, according to Suetonius. Our historian says, " He burned a writer of Atellan farces alive in the middle of the arena of the amphitheater, because of a humorous line of double meaning. When a Roman knight on being thrown to the wild beasts loudly protested his innocence, he took him out, cut off his tongue, and put him back again."

May our American critics be never as fierce as Caligula, and may I not have the will to cut off anybody's tongue in my criticism.

Richard Wilbur

Round About
A Poem of
Housman's

IN THE SPRING OF 1944 MY division was withdrawn from action and assigned to a rest area not far from Naples. Once we had pitched our tents, painted our tent-pegs white, cleaned and polished our equipment, and generally recovered the garrison virtues, we were allowed to make occasional excursions, in groups of one truckload, to nearby points of interest. I remember best our trip to Pompeii. One reason why I remember it so clearly is that, on the day of our visit, Vesuvius began its worst eruption in many decades. Our six-by-six truck approached Pompeii through a fine, steady fall of whitish flakes, and set us down in a square already carpeted with ash. Some of our party, not caring for archeology, headed directly for the bars and other comforts of the modern city; but the rest of us thought it more seemly to begin, at least, with a look at the ruins. We found a displaced Greek woman who offered to be our guide, and she took us through the greater part of the excavations, pointing out the wall paintings, deciphering inscriptions, explaining the water system—until at last, just as we reached the Greek Forum, there was a sudden darkening of the air, a thickening in the fall of ashes, and she took fright and left us.

We found our way back to the modern city and established ourselves in a bar, sitting near the window so that we could watch for the return of our truck. The street was now full of natives evacuating the place, wading through the ashes under the usual clumsy burdens of refugees. Sitting there with a brandy bottle and watching such a scene, we felt something like the final tableau of *Idiot's Delight*. There were jokes about how we had better look smart and sit straight, since we might have to hold our poses for centuries. And one bookish soldier said that he had never felt so close to Pliny the Elder.

Before we had exhausted that vein of nervous humor, the truck arrived, and our scattered party emerged or was extricated from all the bars and dives of the vicinity. Climbing over the tailgate, most of us had some trophy or memento to show or show around: one had a bottle of Marsala, another a bottle of grappa; one had an album of colored views of the ruins; another drew from that breast-pocket which is supposed to carry a bullet-proof New Testament a packet of French postcards. And then there were cameos from Naples, and salamis, and pure silk place-mats marked *Ricordo d'Italia*. When everything had been shown and assessed, one slightly drunken soldier leaned forward on his bench and said, "All right, boys, now you look at *this*." He held out his fist, opened it, and there on his palm stood a small, good replica of the famous sculpture of the wolf, nursing Romulus and Remus.

"How *about* that?" he said. "Man, ain't that the dirtiest got-damn statue you ever saw?"

I don't tell that in ridicule of the soldier who said it. He

had been a good farmer in East Texas, and he was a good soldier
in Italy; his talk had more verve, rhythm, and invention in it—
more poetry in it—than one usually hears in the talk of cultured
people; and I would not call him inferior, as a man, to the soldier
who happened to know that Pliny the Elder was done in by
Vesuvius. I tell the story because, in this hopeful democracy of
ours, in which the most unpromising are coerced into a system
of free public education, we must often remind ourselves that
the art public is not coextensive with the population, or even
with the voting population. Any poet would feel justified in
referring to Romulus and Remus and the wolf—one could hardly
find a classical allusion more safely commonplace; and yet there
really are millions of Americans who would not understand the
reference, and who really might, if they saw the Wolf of the
Capitol, mistake it for a dirty statue. We must stubbornly
remember this whenever polemicists began to strike the Whitman note, and to ask for a poetry at once serious and universally
understandable.

A young Japanese woman told me recently of a parlor game
which she and her friends had often played: fragmentary quotations from haiku are written on slips of paper; the slips of paper
are put into a box; and then each player draws in his turn, reads
out the fragment, and attempts to say the complete seventeen-
syllable poem from memory. When cultured young Japanese
play such a game as that, they are drawing on a detailed acquaintance with a vast haiku literature reaching back more than seven
hundred years. And this acquaintance has to do with far more
than subject matter. Haiku literature is, for instance, full of
plum blossoms; and in order to see the uniqueness of a fragment
having to do with plum blossoms one would have to possess
not only a sense of the total history of that motif in Japanese

verse, but also an intimate familiarity with the norms of diction, the strategies of suggestion and the modes of feeling which belong to the haiku convention and to its great practitioners. It goes without saying that any modern Japanese poet who writes a haiku can expect his best readers to grasp his every echo, variation, or nuance.

It is both good and bad that for American poets and their clientele there exists no such distinct, subtle, and narrow tradition. Our cultural and literary traditions are longer and far more inclusive than the Japanese, but they shape our lives far less decidedly and are subject to perpetual revision. A professor planning the reading list for a freshman Humanities course scratches his head and wonders whether St. Augustine's conception of history is in any way relevant to our own; one critic decides that our present sense of the past can do without Milton and Shelley, while another discovers that the main line of poetic tradition does, after all, lead through Alexander Pope. Similarly, our poets have shifting and rival conceptions of what the "tradition" is, and this leads in practice to a constant renewal, modification, and blending of conventions. What's good about this situation is that our poetry is not conventionally inhibited from coping with modern life as it comes; the modern poem is an adaptable machine that can run on any fuel whatever. The obvious disadvantage is that our unstable sense of literary tradition, and our dissolving multiplicity of conventions, makes it hard for the educated person not a devotee of poetry to develop *tact*.

A tactful person is one who understands not merely what is said, but also what is meant. In a spring issue of the *New Republic*, a correspondent described the melancholy experience of exposing a class of engineers to a well-known four-line poem by Ogden Nash—the one that goes

> Candy
> Is dandy,
> But liquor
> Is quicker.

As I recall, the article said that only one student in the lot recognized that poem as humor. The others either had no response or took it to be a straight-faced admonitory poem about obesity, blood sugar, or some such thing. Now, it is true that contemporary poets, encouraged by the critical rediscovery of the seriousness of wit, have done much to confound the distinction between light verse and serious poetry. Think how light Robert Frost can be, even in a quite serious poem; and think how often Phyllis McGinley trespasses on the serious. Still, it is a terrible failure of tact to read Mr. Nash's poem with a long face. The little jingly lines, the essentially comic rhymes, and the slangy diction combine to require that we place it within the convention of light verse. From a certainty as to the convention we derive a certainty as to tone, and when we know the tone we know what the subject must be: Mr. Nash is writing about strategies of seduction, a topic on which Americans incline to be coy, and his leaving the subject unstated is equivalent to a wink and a dig in the ribs.

Even in poems where the subject is fully stated, there is a world of difference between what is said and what is meant, and this I should like to prove by a brief absurd example. There is a charming popular song called "Paper Moon," the first eight bars of which go as follows:

> Say, it's only a paper moon
> Sailing over a cardboard sea
> But it wouldn't be make believe
> If you believed in me

I want now to juxtapose those lines with a passage from Matthew Arnold's "Dover Beach." That poem begins, as you'll remember,

> The sea is calm tonight,
> The tide is full, the moon lies fair
> Upon the straits . . .

and then it proceeds toward this climactic passage:

> Ah, love, let us be true
> To one another! for the world, which seems
> To lie before us like a land of dreams,
> So various, so beautiful, so new,
> Hath really neither joy, nor love, nor light,
> Nor certitude, nor peace, nor help for pain.

It would be possible, I submit, to compose a one-sentence paraphrase which would do for both "Paper Moon" and "Dover Beach." It might go something like this: "The lover begs his beloved to cleave to him, and thus alleviate through human love his painful sense of the meaninglessness of the modern world, here symbolized by the false beauty of the moon." What I have just done is scandalous, of course; but I hope you will agree that it proves something. It proves that if we consider statement only, and work upon it with the disfiguring tool of paraphrase, a frisky pop-song and a tragic poem can be made to seem identical. From this one can see how much of the meaning of any poem resides in its sound, its pacing, its diction, its literary references, its convention—in all those things which we must apprehend by tact.

One of my favorite poems of A. E. Housman is called "Epitaph on an Army of Mercenaries," and because it is a soluble problem in tact I want to discuss it here. Let me say it to you a first time in a fairly flat voice, so as to stress by *lack* of stress

the necessity, at certain points, of making crucial decisions as
to tone:

> These, in the day when heaven was falling,
> The hour when earth's foundations fled,
> Followed their mercenary calling,
> And took their wages and are dead.
>
> Their shoulders held the sky suspended;
> They stood, and earth's foundations stay;
> What God abandoned, these defended,
> And saved the sum of things for pay.

Perhaps the main decision to be made is, how to say those
last two words, "for pay." Should they be spoken in a weary
drawl? Should they be spoken matter-of-factly? Or should they
be spat out defiantly, as if one were saying "Of *course* they did
it for pay; what did you expect?" Two or three years ago, I
happened to mention Housman's poem to a distinguished author
who is usually right about things, and he spoke very ill of it.
He found distasteful what he called its easy and sweeping
cynicism, and he thought it no better, except in technique, than
the more juvenile pessimistic verses of Stephen Crane. For him,
the gist of the poem was this: "What a stinking world this is,
in which what we call civilization must be preserved by the
blood of miserable hirelings." And for him, that last line was
to be said in a tone of wholesale scorn:

> And saved the *sum of things* for *pay*.

I couldn't accept that way of taking the poem, even though
at the time I was unprepared to argue against it; and so I persisted in saying Housman's lines to myself, in my own way,
while walking or driving or waiting for trains. Then one day I
came upon an excellent essay by Cleanth Brooks, which sup-

ported my notion of the poem and expressed its sense and tone
far better than I could have done. Mr. Brooks likened Housman's Shropshire lads, so many of whom are soldiers, to those
Hemingway heroes who do the brave thing not out of a high
idealism but out of stoic courage and a commitment to some
personal or professional code. Seen in this manner, Housman's
mercenaries—his professional soldiers, that is—are not cynically
conceived; rather their poet is praising them for doing what they
had engaged to do, for doing what had to be done, and for doing
it without a lot of lofty talk. If we understand the poem so, it
is not hard to see what tones and emphases are called for:

> *These*, in the day when heaven was falling
> The hour when earth's foundations fled,
> Followed their mercenary calling,
> And took their wages and are dead.
>
> *Their* shoulders held the sky suspended;
> *They stood*, and earth's foundations stay;
> What God abandoned, *these defended*,
> And saved the sum of things for pay.

That is how I would read it, and I suspect that Mr. Brooks
would concur. But now suppose that the distinguished author
who thought the poem wholly cynical should not be satisfied.
Suppose he should say, "Mr. Brooks' interpretation is very
enhancing, and makes the poem far less cheaply sardonic; but
unfortunately Mr. Brooks is being more creative than critical,
and the poem is really just what I said it was."

There are a number of arguments I might venture in reply,
and one would be this: Housman was a great classical scholar,
and would have been particularly well acquainted with the
convention of the military epitaph. His title refers us, in fact,

to such poems as Simonides wrote in honor of the Spartans who fell at Thermopylae, or the Athenians who fought at the Isthmus. Those poems are celebratory in character, and so is Housman's. The sound and movement of Housman's poem accord, moreover, with the mood of plain solemnity which the convention demands. The tetrameter, which inclines by its nature to skip a bit, and which we have already encountered in "Oh, it's only a paper moon," is slowed down here to the pace of a dead-march. The rhetorical balancing of line against line, and half-line against half-line, the frequency of grammatical stops, and the even placement of strong beats, make a deliberate movement inescapable; and this deliberate movement releases the full and powerful sonority which Housman intends. It is not the music of sardony.

The distinguished author might come back at me here, saying something like this: "No doubt you've named the right convention, but what you forget is that there are *mock*-versions of every convention, including this one. While Housman's mock-use of the military epitaph is not broadly comic but wryly subtle, it does employ the basic trick of high burlesque. Just as Pope, in his mock-epic *The Rape of the Lock*, adopts the tone and matter of Milton or Homer only to deflate them, so Housman sets his solemn, sonorous poem to leaking with the word 'mercenary,' and in the last line lets the air out completely. The poem is thus a gesture of total repudiation, a specimen of indiscriminate romantic irony, and it's what we might expect from the poet who counsels us to 'endure an hour and see injustice done,' who refers to God as 'whatever brute and blackguard made the world,' and who disposes of this life by crying, 'Oh, why did I awake? When shall I sleep again?'"

From now on I am going to play to win, and I shall not allow the distinguished author any further rebuttals. The answer to what he said just now is this: while Housman may maintain that "heaven and earth ail from the prime foundation," he consistently honors those who face up manfully to a bad world; and especially he honors the common soldier who, without having any fancy reasons for doing so, draws his mercenary "thirteen pence a day" and fights and dies. We find this soldier in such poems as "Lancer," or "Grenadier," and Housman always says to him,

> dead or living, drunk or dry,
> Soldier, I wish you well.

The mercenaries of the poem I've been discussing are enlisted from all these other soldier-poems, and though their deaths exemplify the world's evil, Housman stresses not that but the shining of their courage in the general darkness.

The poem is not a mock-version of the military epitaph; however, the distinguished author was right in feeling that Housman's poem is not so free of irony as, for instance, William Collins' eighteenth-century ode, "How sleep the brave . . ." These eight short lines do, in fact, carry a huge freight of irony, most of it implicit in a system of subtle echoes and allusions; but none of the irony is at the expense of the mercenaries, and all of it defends them against slight and detraction.

If one lets the eye travel over Housman's lines, looking for echo or allusion, it is probably line 4 which first arrests the attention:

> And took their wages and are dead.

This puts one in mind of St. Paul's Epistle to the Romans, Chapter VI, where the Apostle declares that "the wages of sin is death." The implication of this echo is that paid professional

soldiers are sinful and unrighteous persons, damned souls who
have forfeited the gift of eternal life. That is certainly not
Housman's view, even if one makes allowance for ironic exaggeration; and so we are forced to try and imagine a sort of person
whose view it might be. The sort of person we're after is, of
course, self-righteous, idealistic, and convinced of his moral
superiority to those common fellows who fight, not for high and
noble reasons, but because fighting is their job. Doubtless you've
heard regulars of the American army subjected to just that kind
of spiritual snobbery, and one readily finds analogies in other
departments of life: think of the way professional politicians are
contemned by our higher-minded citizens, while shiny-faced
amateurs are prized for their wholesome incapacity. Spiritual
snobs are unattractive persons under any circumstances, but they
appear to especial disadvantage in Housman's poem. After all,
they and their civilization were saved by the mercenaries—or
professionals—who did their fighting for them, and that fact
makes their scorn seem both ungrateful and hypocritical.

   Housman's echo of St. Paul, then, leads us to imagine a class
of people who look down on Tommy Atkins, and it also prompts
us to defend Tommy Atkins against their unjust disdain. Let
me turn now to some other echoes, to a number of Miltonic
reverberations which are scattered throughout the poem. They
all derive from some ten lines of the Sixth Book of *Paradise
Lost*. That is the book about the war in heaven, wherein the
good angels and the rebel angels fight two great and inconclusive
engagements, after which the Messiah enters and single-handedly
drives the rebels over the wall of heaven. It is probably not
irrelevant to mention that the ruling idea of Book VI, the idea
which all the action illustrates, is that might derives from right,
and that righteousness therefore must prevail. Here is a passage

which comes at the end of the second battle, when the good and
bad angels are throwing mountains at each other:

> . . . horrid confusion heapt
> Upon confusion rose: and now all Heav'n
> Had gone to wrack, with ruin overspread,
> Had not th' Almighty Father where he sits
> Shrin'd in his Sanctuary of Heav'n secure,
> Consulting on the sum of things, foreseen
> This tumult, and permitted all, advis'd (668 ff.).

The sum of things means here the entire universe, including
heaven and hell, and God is about to save the sum of things
by sending his son against the rebel angels. Otherwise heaven
might fall, and earth's foundations might flee. When the
Messiah drives Satan and his forces over heaven's edge, and they
begin their nine-day fall into hell, Milton gives us another
passage which Housman has echoed:

> Hell heard the unsufferable noise, Hell saw
> Heav'n ruining from Heav'n, and would have fled
> Affrighted; but strict Fate had cast too deep
> Her dark foundations, and too fast had bound (867 ff.).

It's quite plain that Housman is reminding his reader of
Milton, and in particular of these two passages from Book VI, in
which we find "the sum of things," fleeing foundations, and
heaven in peril of falling. The ticklish question now is, how
much of Milton should we put into Housman's poem; how
detailed a comparison should we draw between the war in
Milton's heaven and the battle in which Housman's mercenaries
died? Should we, for instance, compare Housman's sacrificial
mercenaries, whose deaths have preserved the sum of things,
to the Son of God who won the war in heaven and later died

on earth to save mankind? Housman is quite capable of implying
such a comparison. In his poem "The Carpenter's Son," Christ
is a Shropshire lad who dies on the gallows because he would
not "leave ill alone." And in the poem " 1887," Housman says
this of the soldiers who have helped God save the Queen by
dying in battle:

> To skies that knit their heartstrings right,
> To fields that bred them brave,
> The saviours come not home to-night:
> Themselves they could not save.

As Mr. Brooks points out in his essay, those last lines "echo
the passage in the Gospels in which Christ, hanging on the
cross, is taunted with the words: 'Others he saved; himself
he cannot save.'" It appears, then, that in his "Epitaph on an
Army of Mercenaries" Housman may be bestowing on his
soldiers the ultimate commendation; he may be saying that their
sacrifice, in its courage and in the scope of its consequences, was
Christlike. For the rest, I should say that Housman's Miltonic
allusions have a clear derogatory purpose, and that their function
is once again to mock those who feel superior to the soldiers
whom the poet wishes to praise. Housman mocks those who
feel that they are on the side of the angels, that their enemies
are devils, that God is their property and will defend the right,
that heaven and earth depend upon their ascendancy and the
prevalence of their lofty mores, yet who count in fact not on
God or on themselves but on the courage of mercenaries whom
they despise.

These smug people, whom the poem nowhere mentions but
everywhere rebukes, are covertly attacked again in line five
through an allusion to the eleventh labor of Heracles. In that

enterprise, Heracles was out to secure the golden apples of the Hesperides, and he applied for the help of Atlas, the giant who supports the heavens on his shoulders. Atlas agreed to go and get the apples, if Heracles would temporarily take over his burden. When Atlas returned, he noticed that Heracles was supporting the heavens very capably, and it occurred to him that Heracles might well continue in the assignment. Had Heracles not then thought of a good stratagem, and tricked Atlas into reassuming the weight of the skies, he would have been the victim of the greatest buck-passing trick on record. What Housman is saying by way of this allusion is that the battle of his poem was won not on the playing fields of Eton but in the pastures of Shropshire, and that the Etonians, and the other pillars of the established order, transferred their burden in this case to the lowly professional army. Once we recognize Housman's reference, we can see again the extent of his esteem for the so-called mercenaries: he compares them to the great Heracles. And once we perceive that line five has to do with buck-passing, with the transference of a burden, we know where to place the emphasis. It should fall on the first word:

Their shoulders held the sky suspended.

It was *they*, the mercenaries, and not the presumptive upholders of the right, who saved the day.

It seems to me that quite enough allusions have now been found; there may be others, but if so we don't need them for purposes of understanding. Nor, I think, do we need to consider the possible fiscal overtones of the words " saved " and " sum." It's true that in conjunction with the words " wages " and " pay," the phrase " saved the sum " has a slight clink of money in it, and one could probably think up an appropriate meaning

for such a play on words. But readers and critics must be careful
not to be cleverer than necessary; and there is no greater obtuse-
ness than to treat all poets as Metaphysicals, and to insist on
discovering puns which are not likely to be there.

What I've been trying to illustrate, no doubt too exhaustively,
is how a reader might employ tact in arriving at a sure sense of
an eight-line poem. Probably I've gone wrong here or there:
I'm afraid, for one thing, that I've made the poem seem more
English and less universal than it is. But I hope at any rate
to have considered some of the things which need considering:
the convention of the poem; the use of the convention; the
sound, pace, and tone of the poem; its consistency with the
author's attitudes and techniques in other poems; and the implicit
argument of its allusions or echoes. Let me read it a last time:

> These, in the day when heaven was falling,
> The hour when earth's foundations fled,
> Followed their mercenary calling,
> And took their wages and are dead.
>
> Their shoulders held the sky suspended;
> They stood, and earth's foundations stay;
> What God abandoned, these defended,
> And saved the sum of things for pay.

Karl Shapiro has lately published in *Poetry* magazine a prose
outburst with which I greatly sympathize and yet thoroughly
disagree. I won't aim to answer it as a whole, because as he
himself says it is too inconsistent to constitute a clear target.
You can, within limits, argue with a wild man; wild men are
simple; but there's no arguing with a subtle and reasonable man
who is bent on being wild. Let me, however, quote one passage
from Mr. Shapiro which bears on what I've been saying. He
objects to the fact that in our country

the only poetry that is recognized is the poetry that repeats the past, that is referential. It relates back to books, to other poetry, to names in the encyclopaedia. It is the poetry of the history-inhibited mind only, and as such it is meaningless to people who lack the training to read it. The Little Magazine, the avant-gardist, the culture academician base the esthetic experience on education. Whereas poetry needs not education or culture but the open perceptions of the healthy human organism.

Mr. Shapiro and I agree that a poem which refers to Romulus and Remus and the wolf will be meaningless, in part at least, to those who lack the training to read it. I disagree, however, with Mr. Shapiro's determination to hound that wolf out of poetry, to abolish the literary and historical past, to confine us to the modern city and declare the ruins off-limits. It would not be worth it to make poetry more generally usable at the cost of abridging the poet's consciousness.

I will say, parenthetically, that I wish the category of expertly-made popular poetry had not all but disappeared in this century. In the last century, the best poets did not hesitate to write on occasion simple songs, hymns, or story-poems which were instantly possessed and valued by a larger public. The author of "In Memoriam" also wrote the ballad of "The Revenge." Though societies were formed to unravel the knottier verses of Robert Browning, there are no knots in "The Pied Piper of Hamelin." I think too of James Russell Lowell's "Once to Every Man and Nation," and of Longfellow's "Paul Revere." These are all fine poems, and all of them are perfectly transparent. Perhaps it is their very transparency which has led critics and teachers to fall silent about them, there being no call for learned mediation; and perhaps that silence has helped many of our poets to forget that there is such a thing as a good popular poem.

But now let me take Housman's poem as a miniature specimen of what Mr. Shapiro calls "high art," and defend it against Mr. Shapiro. It is probably not Housman whom Mr. Shapiro is attacking, and yet the strictures might all apply to him. Mr. Shapiro talks as if a poem could be either referential or humanly vital, but not both. Surely you will agree that Housman's poem is both: it is a passionate celebration of courage, prompted one suspects by an immediate occasion; at the same time, and without any dampening of its urgency, it recalls a convention as old as the Greeks, and defends its heroes against detraction through liberal allusions to literature and myth. Mr. Shapiro says that to be referential is to "repeat the past"; Housman most certainly does not do that. What he does is to confront the present with a mind and heart which contain the past. His poem does not knuckle under to a Greek convention, it makes use of that convention and much modifies it. His allusions do not "repeat" Milton and St. Paul, they bring them to bear upon a contemporary event, and in turn they bring that event to bear upon Milton and St. Paul. Milton's good angels are not, in Housman's poem, what they were in *Paradise Lost*; they are transformed by a fresh conjunction; and Housman implicitly quarrels both with the moral exclusiveness of St. Paul and with Milton's idea that righteousness must prevail.

I would uphold Housman's poem as a splendid demonstration of the art of referring. The poem requires a literate reader, but given such a reader it is eminently effective. I selected the poem for discussion precisely because, unlike most of Housman, it is capable of misinterpretation; nevertheless, as I've pointed out, a reader *can* arrive at a just sense of its tone and drift without consciously identifying any of its references. It *all but* delivers its whole meaning right away. One reason why Housman's allusions can be slow in transpiring, as they were for me, is that the words which point toward Milton or St. Paul—such words as "wages" or "earth's foundations"—are perfectly at home in the language of the poem as a whole; and this seems to me a great virtue. In a bad poem, there are often certain words which step out of line, wave their arms, and cry "Follow me! I have overtones!" It takes a master to make references, or what Robert Frost calls "displacements," without in any way falsifying the poem's voice, its way of talking. Now, as for the allusions proper, they are to the Bible, *Paradise Lost*, and Greek mythology, all of which are central to *any* version of our tradition, and in some degree familiar to every educated reader. So familiar are these sources that I'm sure Housman's allusions must unconsciously affect anyone's understanding of the poem, even upon a casual first reading. And I would say that our familiarity with the things to which Housman is referring justifies the subtlety and brevity of his echoes. The poem assumes that the words "wages" and "dead" will suffice to suggest St. Paul, and I think that a fair assumption.

Housman's allusions, once one is aware of them, are not decorative but very hard working. Their chief function is to supplement Housman's explicit praise of the mercenaries with implicit dispraise of their detractors, and so make us certain of the poem's whole attitude toward its subject. To achieve such certainty, however, one need not catch every hint, every echo; any *one* of Housman's references, rightly interpreted, will permit the reader to take confident possession of the poem. I like that. A poem should not be like a double-crostic; it should not be the sort of puzzle in which you get nothing until you get it all. Art doesn't or shouldn't work that way; we are not cheated of a symphony if we fail to react to some passage on the flute, and a good poem should yield itself more than once, offering the reader an early and sure purchase, and deepening repeatedly as he comes to know it better.

This is what happens time and again as one reads and re-reads Housman. In his poem, "On the Idle Hill of Summer," an indolent young man hears the stirring and fatal music of a marching column, and decides to enlist. The final quatrain goes like this:

> Far the calling bugles hollo,
> High the screaming fife replies,
> Gay the files of scarlet follow;
> Woman bore me, I will rise.

"Woman bore me, I will rise." He will rise and enlist because "woman bore him"—that is, because he is a man and can't resist the summons of the bugle. The last line is forceful and plain, and clinches the poem beautifully. We need no more. Yet there is more, and perhaps on the second reading, or the fifth, or the twentieth, we may hear in that last line a reverberation of the prayer which is said at the graveside in the Anglican burial service, and which begins: "Man, that is born of a woman, hath but a short time to live, and is full of misery . . ."

If we do catch that echo, the line gains both in power and in point; but if we don't catch it, we are still possessed of a complete and trustworthy version of Housman's poem. And to speak again of Milton, I think that most of the reverberations in *Paradise Lost* work in the same way. Satan, wakening in the fiery gulf of Hell, says to Beelzebub, who is sprawled at his side:

If thou beest he; But O how fall'n! how chang'd
From him, who in the happy Realms of Light
Cloth'd with transcendent brightness didst outshine
Myriads though bright . . .

There is a suggestion of Isaiah there which perhaps I might
notice unassisted; but I lack the ready knowledge of Virgil which
Milton reasonably expected of his reader, and so I am grateful
for the scholar's footnote which directs me to Book II of the
Aeneid. There the shade of Hector appears to Aeneas in a
dream, mangled, blackened with dirt, and *quantum mutatus ab
illo Hectore*—" how changed " from that Hector who once returned from battle clothed in the bright armor of Achilles! The
Virgilian echo is enhancing; it helps to tune the voice of Satan,
and the likening of Beelzebub to Hector poignantly stresses the
rebel angels' fall from brightness and from heroic strength and
virtue. But if there were no footnote to help me, if I never
sensed the shade of Hector behind Milton's lines, I should not
on that account be balked or misled. I should already have
gathered from the surface of the lines one sure and adequate
sense of their tone and meaning.

Let me now read you a more dubious example of the art of
referring. The poem is by Yeats; it was written in 1909 or
1910, after the poet's reconciliation with Maud Gonne; and its
title is " King and No King."

"Would it were anything but merely voice!"
The No King cried who after that was King,
Because he had not heard of anything
That balanced with a word is more than noise;
Yet Old Romance being kind, let him prevail
Somewhere or somehow that I have forgot,
Though he'd but cannon—Whereas we that had thought

To have lit upon as clean and sweet a tale
Have been defeated by that pledge you gave
In momentary anger long ago;
And I that have not your faith, how shall I know
That in the blinding light beyond the grave
We'll find so good a thing as that we have lost?
The hourly kindness, the day's common speech,
The habitual content of each with each
When neither soul nor body has been crossed.

A great many intelligent readers, including some professional poets of my acquaintance, have found this poem very troublesome. In order to fathom its sixteen lines, one must follow the suggestion of Yeats' title and read *A King and No King*, which is a five-act play by Beaumont and Fletcher first performed in 1611. The play tells how King Arbaces of Iberia conceives an incestuous passion for his sister Panthea, and how his apparently hopeless situation is at last happily resolved by the discovery that Panthea is, after all, *not* his sister. Prior to this fifth-act clarification, Arbaces delivers a number of violent speeches expressing thwarted lust, and one of these Yeats has quoted. Speaking of the words " brother " and " sister," which are the obstacles to his seemingly guilty passion, Arbaces cries, " Let 'em be anything but merely voice "—meaning that if only they were not bodiless words, but concrete things like soldiers or cities, he could turn his cannon on them and destroy them.

Yeats is comparing King Arbaces' frustrated desires to his own, and he is also comparing the words " brother " and " sister," which so vex Arbaces, to some unshakeable pledge or vow made by the lady who is the addressee of his poem. If we look into Richard Ellmann's biography of Yeats, we find that Maud Gonne, in 1909, had informed Yeats " that their relations could be those of a spiritual marriage only," and that she had assured him, "You will not suffer because I will pray." Once we have this information, Yeats' poem becomes perfectly clear: it is a plea for physical as well as spiritual love, and in re-reading it we must put a strong emphasis on the word "body" in the last line.

When one has managed to figure out some puzzling poem, it is natural to be a little foolishly proud; one feels like an insider, an initiate, and one is not inclined to be very critical of a work which has certified one's cleverness and industry. For a few heady weeks in 1954, I thought of myself as the only living understander of Yeats' "King and No King." Since then, however, the number of insiders has grown considerably, and I now feel less proprietary toward the poem, and more objective. There is much to admire in "King and No King": the rhythmic movement is splendidly dramatic; the language slides deftly in and out of the common idiom; in respect of pacing and diction, the poem is a good specimen of that artful recklessness, that *sprezzatura*, which Yeats was aiming at in the first decade of this century. Yet what an inconsistency there is between the blurting, spontaneous manner of the opening lines, and the poet's stubborn withholding of the theme! A good poet knows how, in referring to some little-known thing, to convey without loss of concision some sense of what the reference *must* mean; but Yeats, though he devotes almost seven lines to the Beaumont and Fletcher play, chooses to suppress any suggestion whatever that the play, and his poem, are concerned with frustrated sexual appetite. The consequence is that the reader stumbles badly on the sill of the poem, and never stops staggering until he is out the back door.

There are reasons, I suspect, for Yeats' having used a remote literary reference not only as a source of analogies to his personal

predicament, but also as a means of enshrouding his subject
matter. The subject is, after all, inherently delicate, and there
is also some danger of the ridiculous in an argumentative plea
for physical favors, especially if one has known the woman since
the late 1880's. But whatever Yeats' reasons for writing as he
did—and I have no real business guessing at them—one must
wonder about the public value of a poem which mutes its theme
by a thoroughly reticent allusion to a little-known text. One
must also question the integrity, the artistic self-sufficiency, of
any short poem which requires to be grasped through the
reading of a bad five-act play and the consultation of a biography.

As the English critic John Press recently said, "There is a
popular belief that what conservatives like to call real poetry
was perfectly straightforward until some unspecified date, when
poets suddenly changed into reckless bunglers or deliberately
set out to bamboozle plain, honest readers with mumbo-jumbo."
I hope that I don't seem to be offering aid and comfort to the
holders of that unhistorical belief. What I do mean to say, in
concession to Mr. Shapiro's view of things, is that the art of
reference in poetry has become a very difficult art, owing to the
incoherence of our culture, and that some poems refer more
successfully than others. It is generally agreed, I hope, that one
cannot sensibly describe a poem as a direct message from poet
to public; but one can say that a poem addresses itself, in I. A.
Richards' phrase, to some "condition of the language," and
presupposes some condition of the culture. Every poem is based
on an unformulated impression of what words and things are
known and valued in the literate community; every poem is
written, as it were, in some intellectual and cultural key. It
is therefore possible to say of a poem that, in relation to its
appropriate audience, it is tactful or not.

Housman's poem is a model of tact, both in its references and in its manner of referring. Yeats' poem is less tactful, because it cites an ancient play which the most eligible and cultured reader might not know, and which must be known if the poem is to be breached at all. As for the *Cantos* of Ezra Pound, they contain some of the finest passages in modern poetry, but they are supremely tactless. That is, they seem to arise from a despair of any community, and they do not imply a possible audience as Housman's poem does. It is all very well for Pound to claim that his *Cantos* deal " with the usual subjects of conversation between intelligent men "; but intelligent men, though they do talk of history and economics and the arts, do not converse in broken fragments of mythology, unattributed quotations, snatches of Renaissance correspondence, cryptic reminiscences, and bursts of unorthodox Chinese. Pound's presentational manner of writing, which developed out of Imagism, is the method least capable of turning his eccentric erudition into a consistently usable poetry. The advantage of the method is immediacy, and the investment of the idea in the thing, but the method does not work unless the reader knows what it is that is being so immediate. Because the *Cantos* lack any discursive tissue, because they refuse the reader any sort of intercession, even those whose learning exceeds Ezra Pound's cannot be said to be ready for them.

There are three things a reader might do about the *Cantos*. First, he might decide not to read them. Second, he might read them as Dr. Williams recommends, putting up with much bafflement for the sake of the occasional perfect lyric, the consistently clean and musical language, and the masterly achievement of quantitative effects through the strophic balancing of rhythmic masses. Or, thirdly, the reader might decide to understand the

Cantos by consulting, over a period of years, the many books
from which Pound drew his material. At almost every university,
nowadays, there is someone who has undertaken that task: he
may be identified by the misshapenness of his learning and by
his air of lost identity.

None of the three courses I have mentioned is a thoroughly
happy one, and the *Cantos* are one proof of Mr. Shapiro's
contention that poetry's relations with the past, on the one hand,
and with its public on the other, have become problematical.
I will grant Mr. Shapiro that there are misuses of the past which
can be hurtful to poetry. Antiquarianism is one: the rapt
pedantry of Ezra Pound, and the bland, donnish pedantry of
certain other poets, alike distract us from the uninterpreted fields
and streets and rooms of the present, in which the real battles
of imagination must be fought. I will grant, too, that the sense
of history can be crippling to poetry if history is so interpreted
as to impose some narrow limitation or imperative on the poet.
The poet must not feel dwarfed by the literary past, nor should
he listen too trustingly to those who say that poetry's role in
society is inevitably diminishing. Nor should he adjust his
concerns to what others consider the great thought-currents of
the times: the *Zeitgeist*, after all, is only a spook invented by
the critics. Nor, finally, does poetry prosper when it puts itself
wholly at the service of some movement, some institution. I
think of Mayakovsky, who wrote " I have subdued myself, setting
my heel on the throat of my own song," and who said that he
had "cancelled out his soul" the better to serve the socialist
age. It may be true, as some say, that Mayakovsky was made by
the Revolution; but surely the service of history broke him as
well. In all these ways, historical consciousness can paralyze,
trivialize or enslave the poet's art; but I am not on that account

moved to accept Mr. Shapiro's imperative, which is that poets must now secede from history and dwell in "biological time."

The past which most properly concerns the poet is, as T. S. Eliot has said, both temporal and timeless. It is, above all, a great index of human possibilities. It is a dimension in which we behold, and are beheld by, all those forms of excellence and depravity which men have assumed and may assume again. The poet needs this lively past as a means of viewing the present without provinciality, and of saying much in little; he must hope for the tact and the talent to make that past usable for the audience which his poems imply. My friend John Ciardi once said, "Pompeii is everybody's home town, sooner or later." I should add that for every poet, whatever he may say as critic or polemicist, Pompeii is still a busy quarter of the city of imagination.

Randall Jarrell

Robert Frost's

"Home Burial"

"HOME BURIAL" AND "THE Witch of Coös" seem to me the best of all Frost's dramatic poems—though "A Servant to Servants" is nearly as good. All three are poems about women in extreme situations: neurotic or (in "A Servant to Servants") psychotic women. The circumstances of the first half of his life made Frost feel for such women a sympathy or empathy that amounted almost to identification. He said that, "creature of literature that I am," he had learned to "make a virtue of my suffering / From nearly everything that goes on round me," and that "Kit Marlowe taught me how to say my prayers: / 'Why, this is Hell, nor am I out of it.'" It is with such women that he says this—this and more than this: the Pauper Witch of Grafton's

> Up where the trees grow short, the mosses tall,
> I made him gather me wet snow berries
> On slippery rocks beside a waterfall.
> I made him do it for me in the dark.
> And he liked everything I made him do . . .

shows us, as few passages can, that for a while the world was heaven too.

"Home Burial" is a fairly long but extraordinarily concentrated poem; after you have known it long enough you feel almost as the Evangelist did, that if all the things that could be said about it were written down, "I suppose that even the world itself could not contain the books that should be written." I have written down a few of these things; but, first of all, here is "Home Burial" itself:

> He saw her from the bottom of the stairs
> Before she saw him. She was starting down,
> Looking back over her shoulder at some fear.
> She took a doubtful step and then undid it
> To raise herself and look again. He spoke
> Advancing toward her: "What is it you see
> From up there always—for I want to know."
> She turned and sank upon her skirts at that,
> And her face changed from terrified to dull.
> He said to gain time: "What is it you see,"
> Mounting until she cowered under him.
> "I will find out now—you must tell me, dear."
> She, in her place, refused him any help
> With the least stiffening of her neck and silence.
> She let him look, sure that he wouldn't see,
> Blind creature; and awhile he didn't see.
> But at last he murmured, "Oh," and again, "Oh."
>
> "What is it—what?" she said.
>   "Just that I see."
>
> "You don't," she challenged. "Tell me what it is."
>
> "The wonder is I didn't see at once.
> I never noticed it from here before.
> I must be wonted to it—that's the reason.
> The little graveyard where my people are!
> So small the window frames the whole of it.
> Not so much larger than a bedroom, is it?

There are three stones of slate and one of marble,
Broad-shouldered little slabs there in the sunlight
On the sidehill. We haven't to mind *those*.
But I understand: it is not the stones,
But the child's mound—"

                 "Don't, don't, don't, don't," she cried.

She withdrew shrinking from beneath his arm
That rested on the banister, and slid downstairs;
And turned on him with such a daunting look,
He said twice over before he knew himself:
"Can't a man speak of his own child he's lost?"

"Not you! Oh, where's my hat? Oh, I don't need it!
I must get out of here. I must get air.
I don't know rightly whether any man can."

"Amy! Don't go to someone else this time.
Listen to me. I won't come down the stairs."
He sat and fixed his chin between his fists.
"There's something I should like to ask you, dear."

"You don't know how to ask it."

                     "Help me, then."

Her fingers moved the latch for all reply.

"My words are nearly always an offence.
I don't know how to speak of anything
So as to please you. But I might be taught,
I should suppose. I can't say I see how.
A man must partly give up being a man
With women-folk. We could have some arrangement
By which I'd bind myself to keep hands off
Anything special you're a-mind to name.
Though I don't like such things 'twixt those that love.
Two that don't love can't live together without them.
But two that do can't live together with them."
She moved the latch a little. "Don't—don't go.
Don't carry it to someone else this time.

Tell me about it if it's something human.
Let me into your grief. I'm not so much
Unlike other folks as your standing there
Apart would make me out. Give me my chance.
I do think, though, you overdo it a little.
What was it brought you up to think it the thing
To take your mother-loss of a first child
So inconsolably—in the face of love.
You'd think his memory might be satisfied—"

"There you go sneering now!"
                              "I'm not, I'm not!
You make me angry. I'll come down to you.
God, what a woman! And it's come to this,
A man can't speak of his own child that's dead."

"You can't because you don't know how to speak.
If you had any feelings, you that dug
With your own hand—how could you?—his little grave;
I saw you from that very window there
Making the gravel leap and leap in air,
Leap up, like that, like that, and land so lightly
And roll back down the mound beside the hole.
I thought, Who is that man? I didn't know you.
And I crept down the stairs and up the stairs
To look again, and still your spade kept lifting.
Then you came in. I heard your rumbling voice
Out in the kitchen, and I don't know why,
But I went near to see with my own eyes.
You could sit there with the stains on your shoes
Of the fresh earth from your own baby's grave
And talk about your everyday concerns.
You had stood the spade up against the wall
Outside there in the entry, for I saw it."

"I shall laugh the worst laugh I ever laughed.
I'm cursed. God, if I don't believe I'm cursed."

"I can repeat the very words you were saying.
'Three foggy mornings and one rainy day
Will rot the best birch fence a man can build.'
Think of it, talk like that at such a time!
What had how long it takes a birch to rot
To do with what was in the darkened parlor.
You *couldn't* care! The nearest friends can go
With anyone to death, comes so far short
They might as well not try to go at all.
No, from the time when one is sick to death,
One is alone, and he dies more alone.
Friends make pretense of following to the grave,
But before one is in it, their minds are turned
And making the best of their way back to life
And living people, and things they understand.
But the world's evil. I won't have grief so
If I can change it. Oh, I won't, I won't!"

"There, you have said it all and you feel better.
You won't go now. You're crying. Close the door.
The heart's gone out of it: why keep it up.
Amy! There's someone coming down the road!"

"*You*—oh, you think the talk is all. I must go—
Somewhere out of this house. How can I make you—"

"If—you—do!" She was opening the door wider.
"Where do you mean to go? First tell me that.
I'll follow and bring you back by force. I *will!*—"

The poem's first sentence, "He saw her from the bottom
of the stairs / Before she saw him," implies what the poem very
soon states: that, knowing herself seen, she would have acted
differently—she has two sorts of behavior, behavior for him to
observe and spontaneous immediate behavior. "She was starting
down, / Looking back over her shoulder at some fear" says that
it is *some fear*, and not a specific feared object, that she is looking
back at; and, normally, we do not look back over our shoulder

at what we leave, unless we feel for it something more than fear. "She took a doubtful step" emphasizes the queer attraction or fascination that the fear has for her; her departing step is not sure it should depart. "She took a doubtful step and then *undid* it": the surprising use of *undid* gives her withdrawal of the tentative step a surprising reality. The poem goes on: 'To raise herself and look again." It is a little vertical ballet of indecision toward and away from a fearful but mesmerically attractive object, something hard to decide to leave and easy to decide to return to. "He spoke / Advancing toward her": having the old line end with "spoke," the new line begin with "advancing," makes the very structure of the lines express the way in which he looms up, gets bigger. (Five lines later Frost repeats the effect even more forcibly with: "He said to gain time, 'What is it you see,' / Mounting until she cowered under him.") Now when the man asks: "What is it you see / From up there always—for I want to know," the word "always" tells us that all this has gone on many times before, and that he has seen it—without speaking of it—a number of times before. The phrase "for I want to know" is a characteristic example of the heavy, willed demands that the man makes, and an even more characteristic example of the tautological, rhetorical announcements of his actions that he so often makes, as if he felt that the announcement somehow justified or excused the action.

The poem goes on: "She turned and sank upon her skirts at that . . ." The stairs permit her to subside into a modest, compact, feminine bundle; there is a kind of smooth deftness about the phrase, as if it were some feminine saying: "When in straits, sink upon your skirts." The next line, "And her face changed from terrified to dull," is an economically elegant way of showing how the terror of surprise (perhaps with another fear underneath it) changes into the dull lack of response that is her regular mask for him. The poem continues: "He said to gain time"—to gain time in which to think of the next thing to say, to gain time in which to get close to her and gain the advantage of his physical nearness, his physical bulk. His next "What is it you see" is the first of his many repetitions; if one knew only this man one would say, "Man is the animal that repeats." In the poem's next phrase, "mounting until she cowered under him," the identity of the vowels in "mounting" and "cowered" physically connects the two, makes his mounting the plain immediate cause of her cowering. "I will find out now" is another of his rhetorical announcements of what he is going to do: "this time you're going to tell me, I'm going to make you." But this heavy willed compulsion changes into sheer appeal, into reasonable beseeching, in his next phrase: "You must tell me, dear." The "dear" is affectionate intimacy, the "must" is the "must" of rational necessity; yet the underlying form of the sentence is that of compulsion. The poem goes on: "She, in her place, refused him any help . . ." The separated phrase "in her place" describes and embodies, with economical brilliance, both her physical and spiritual lack of outgoingness, forthcomingness; she brims over none of her contours, remains sitting upon her skirts upon her stair-step, in feminine exclusion. "Refused him any help / With the least stiffening of her neck and silence": she doesn't say Yes, doesn't say No, doesn't say; her refusal of any answer is worse than almost any answer. "The least stiffening of her neck," in its concise reserve, its slight precision, is more nearly conclusive than any larger gesture of rejection. He, in extremities, usually repeats some proverbial or rhetorical generalization; at such moments she usually responds either with a particular, specific sentence, or else with something more particular than any sentence: with some motion or gesture.

The next line, "She let him look, sure that he wouldn't see," reminds one of some mother bird so certain that her nest is hidden that she doesn't even flutter off, but sits there on it, risking what is no risk, in complacent superiority. "Sure that he wouldn't see, / Blind creature": the last phrase is quoted from her mind, is her contemptuous summing up. "And a while he didn't see"; but at last when he sees, he doesn't tell her what it is, doesn't silently understand, but with heavy slow comprehension murmurs, "Oh," and then repeats, "Oh." It is another announcement of what he is doing, a kind of dramatic rendition of his understanding. (Sometimes when we are waiting for someone, and have made some sound or motion we are afraid will seem ridiculous to the observer we didn't know was there, we rather ostentatiously look at our watch, move our face and lips into a "What on earth could have happened to make him so late?" as a way of justifying our earlier action. The principle behind our action is the principle behind many of this man's actions.) With the undignified alacrity of someone hurrying to re-establish a superiority that has been questioned, the woman cries out like a child: "What it is—what?" Her sentence is, so to speak, a rhetorical question rather than a real one, since it takes it for granted that a correct answer can't be made. His reply, "Just that I see," shows that his unaccustomed insight has given him an unaccustomed composure; she has had the advantage, for so long, of being the only one who knows, that he for a moment prolongs the advantage of being the only one who knows that he knows. The immediately following "'You don't,' she challenged. 'Tell me what it is,'" is the instant, childishly assertive exclamation of someone whose human position depends entirely upon her knowing what some inferior being can never know; she cannot let another second go by without hearing the incorrect answer that will confirm her in her rightness and superiority.

The man goes on explaining, to himself, and to mankind, and to her too, in slow rumination about it and about it. In his "The wonder is I didn't see at once. / I never noticed it from here before. / I must be wonted to it—that's the reason," one notices how "wonder" and "once" prepare for "wonted," that provincial-, archaic-sounding word that sums up—as "used" never could—his reliance on a habit or accustomedness which at last sees nothing but itself, and hardly sees that; and when it does see something through itself, beyond itself, slowly marvels. In the next line, "The little graveyard where my people are!" we feel not only the triumph of the slow person at last comprehending, but also the tender, easy accustomedness of habit, of long use, of a kind of cosy social continuance—for him the graves are not the healed scars of old agonies, but are something as comfortable and accustomed as the photographs in the family album. "So small the window frames the whole of it," like the later "Broad-shouldered little slabs there in the sunlight / On the sidehill," not only has this easy comfortable acceptance, but also has the regular feel of a certain sort of Frost nature-description: this is almost the only place in the poem where for a moment we feel that it is Frost talking first and the man talking second. But the man's "Not so much larger than a bedroom, is it?"—an observation that appeals to her for agreement—carries this comfortable acceptance to a point at which it becomes intolerable: the only link between the bedroom and the graveyard is the child conceived in their bedroom and buried in that graveyard. The sentence comfortably establishes a connection which she cannot bear to admit the existence of—she tries to keep the two things permanently separated in her mind. (What he says amounts to his saying about their bedroom:

"Not so much smaller than the graveyard, is it?") "There are three stones of slate and one of marble, / Broad-shouldered little slabs there in the sunlight / On the sidehill," has a heavy tenderness and accustomedness about it, almost as if he were running his hand over the grain of the stone. The "little" graveyard and "little" slabs are examples of our regular way of making something acceptable or dear by means of a diminutive.

Next, to show her how well he understands, the man shows her how ill he understands. He says about his family's graves: "We haven't to mind *those*"; that is, we don't have to worry about, grieve over, my people: it is not your obligation to grieve for them at all, nor mine to give them more than their proper share of grief, the amount I long ago measured out and used up. But with the feeling, akin to a sad, modest, relieved, surprised pride, with which he regularly responds to his own understanding, he tells her that he does understand: what matters is not the old stones but the new mound, the displaced earth piled up above the grave which he had dug and in which their child is buried.

When he says this it is as if he had touched, with a crude desecrating hand, the sacred, forbidden secret upon which her existence depends. With shuddering hysterical revulsion she cries: "Don't, don't, don't, don't." (If the reader will compare the effect of Frost's four "don'ts" with the effect of three or five, he will see once more how exactly accurate, perfectly effective, almost everything in the poem is.) The poem continues: "She withdrew shrinking from beneath his arm / That rested on the banister, and slid downstairs"; the word "slid" says, with vivid indecorousness, that anything goes in extremities, that you can't be bothered, then, by mere appearance or propriety; "slid" has the ludicrous force of actual fact, is the way things are instead of the way we agree they are. In the line "And turned on him with such a daunting look," the phrase "turned on him" makes her resemble a cornered animal turning on its pursuer; and "with such a daunting look" is the way he phrases it to himself, is quoted from his mind as "blind creature" was quoted from hers. The beautifully provincial, old-fashioned, folk-sounding "daunting" reminds one of the similar, slightly earlier "wonted," and seems to make immediate, as no other word could, the look that cows him. The next line, "He said twice over before he knew himself," tells us that repetition, saying something twice over, is something he regresses to under stress; unless he can consciously prevent himself from repeating, he repeats. What he says twice over (this is the third time already that he has repeated something) is a rhetorical question, a querulous, plain-tive appeal to public opinion: "Can't a man speak of his own child he's lost?" He does not say specifically, particularly, with confidence in himself: "I've the right to speak of our dead child"; instead he cites the acknowledged fact that any member of the class *man* has the acknowledged right to mention, just to mention, that member of the class of his belongings, *his own child*—and he has been unjustly deprived of this right. "His own child he's lost" is a way of saying: "You act as if he were just yours, but he's just as much just mine; that's an established fact." "Can't a man speak of his own child he's lost" has a magnificently dissonant, abject, aggrieved querulousness about it, in all its sounds and all its rhythms; "Can't a man" prepares us for the even more triumphantly ugly dissonance (or should I say consonance?) of the last two words in her "I don't know rightly whether any man can."

Any rhetorical question demands, expects, the hearer's auto-matic agreement; there is nothing it expects less than a particular, specific denial. The man's "Can't a man speak . . ." means "Isn't any man allowed to speak . . . ," but her fatally specific answer, "Not you!" makes it mean, "A man cannot—is not able to—speak, if the man is you." Her "Oh, where's my hat?" is a speech accompanied by action, means: "I'm leaving. Where's the hat which social convention demands that a respectable woman put on, to go out into the world?" The immediately following "Oh, I don't need it!" means: in extremities, in cases when we come down to what really matters, what does social convention or respectability really matter? Her "I must get out of here. I must get air," says that you breathe understanding and suffocate without it, and that in this house, for her, there is none. Then, most extraordinarily, she gives a second specific answer to his rhetorical question, that had expected none: "I don't know rightly whether any man can." The line says: "Perhaps it is not the individual *you* that's to blame, but man in general; perhaps a woman is wrong to expect that any man can speak—really *speak*—of his dead child."

His "Amy! Don't go to someone else this time" of course tells us that another time she *has* gone to someone else; and it tells us the particular name of this most particular woman, something that she and the poem never tell us about the man. The man's "Listen to me. I won't come down the stairs" tells us that earlier he *has* come down the stairs, hasn't kept his distance. It (along with "shrinking," "cowered," and many later things in the poem) tells us that he has given her reason to be physically afraid of him; his "I won't come down the stairs" is a kind of euphemism for "I won't hurt you, won't even get near you."

The poem's next sentence, "He sat and fixed his chin between his fists"—period, end of line—with its four short *i*'s, its "fixed" and "fists," fixes him in baffled separateness; the sentence fits into the line as he fits into the isolated perplexity of his existence. Once more he makes a rhetorical announcement of what he is about to do, before he does it: "There's something I should

like to ask you, dear." The sentence tiptoes in, gentle, almost
abjectly mollifying, and ends with a reminding "dear"; it is
an indirect rhetorical appeal that expects for an answer at least
a grudging: "Well, go ahead and ask it, then." His sentence
presupposes the hearer's agreement with what it implies: "Anyone is at least allowed to *ask*, even if afterward you refuse him
what he asks." The woman once more gives a direct, crushing,
particular answer: "You don't know how to ask it." "Anyone
may be allowed to ask, but *you* are not because you are not able
to ask"; we don't even need to refuse an animal the right to
ask and be refused, since if we gave him the right he couldn't
exercise it. The man's "Help me, then," has an absolute,
almost abject helplessness, a controlled childlike simplicity,
that we pity and sympathize with; yet we can't help remem-
bering the other side of the coin, the heavy, brutal, equally
simple and helpless anger of his later *I'll come down to you*.

The next line, "Her fingers moved the latch for all reply"
(like the earlier "She refused him any help / With the least
stiffening of her neck and silence"; like "She turned on him
with such a daunting look"; like the later "She moved the latch
a little"; like the last "She was opening the door wider"),
reminds us that the woman has a motion-language more immediate, direct, and particular than words—a language she resorts
to in extremities, just as he, in extremities, resorts to a language
of repeated proverbial generalizations. "Home Burial" starts
on the stairs but continues in the doorway, on the threshold
between the old life inside and the new life outside.

The man now begins his long appeal with the slow, heavy,
hopeless admission that "My words are nearly always an offence."
This can mean, "Something is nearly always wrong with me
and my words," but it also can mean—does mean, underneath—
that she is to be blamed for nearly always finding offensive

things that certainly are not meant to offend. "I don't know how to speak of anything / So as to please you" admits, sadly blames himself for, his baffled ignorance, but it also suggests that she is unreasonably, fantastically hard to please—if the phrase came a little later in his long speech he might pronounce it "so as to please *you*." (Whatever the speaker intends, there are no long peacemaking speeches in a quarrel; after a few sentences the speaker always has begun to blame the other again.) The man's aggrieved, blaming "But I might be taught, I should suppose" is followed by the helpless, very endearing admission: "I can't say I see how"; for the moment this removes the blame from her, and his honesty of concession makes us unwilling to blame him. He tries to summarize his dearly-bought understanding in a generalization, almost a proverb: "A man must partly give up being a man / With women-folk." The sentence begins in the dignified regretful sunlight of the main floor, in "A man must partly give up being a man," and ends huddled in the basement below, in "With women-folk." He doesn't use the parallel, co-ordinate "with a woman," but the entirely different "with women-folk"; the sentence tries to be fair and objective, but it is as completely weighted a sentence as "A man must partly give up being a man / With the kiddies," or "A man must partly give up being a man / With Bandar-log." The sentence presupposes that the real right norm is a man being a man with men, and that some of this rightness and normality always must be sacrificed with that special case, that inferior anomalous category, "women-folk."

He goes on: "We could have some arrangement [it has a hopeful, indefinite, slightly helter-skelter sound] / By which I'd bind myself to keep hands off"—the phrases "bind myself" and "keep hands off" have the primitive, awkward materiality of someone taking an oath in a bad saga; we expect the sentence to end in some awkwardly impressive climax, but get the almost ludicrous anticlimax of "Anything special you're a-mind to name." And, too, the phrase makes whatever she names quite willful on her part, quite unpredictable by reasonable man. His sensitivity usually shows itself to be a willing, hopeful form of insensitivity, and he himself realizes this here, saying: "Though I don't like such things 'twixt those that love." Frost then makes him express his own feeling in a partially truthful but elephantine aphorism that lumbers, through a queerly stressed line a foot too long ("Two that don't love can't live together without them") into a conclusion ("But two that do can't live together with them") that has some of the slow, heavy relish just in being proverbial that the man so often shows. (How hard it is to get through the monosyllables of the two lines!) His words don't convince her, and she replies to them without words: "She moved the latch a little." He repeats in grieved appeal: "Don't—don't go. / Don't carry it to someone else this time." (He is repeating an earlier sentence, with "don't go" changed to "don't carry it.") The next line, "Tell me about it if it's something human," is particularly interesting when it comes from him. When is something inside a human being not human, so that it can't be told? Isn't it when it is outside man's understanding, outside all man's categories and pigeonholes—when there is no proverb to say for it? It is, then, a waste or abyss impossible to understand or manage or share with another. His next appeal to her, "Let me into your grief," combines an underlying sexual metaphor with a child's "Let me in! let me in!" This man who is so much a member of the human community feels a helpless bewilderment at being shut out of the little group of two of which he was once an anomalous half; the woman has put in the place of this group, a group of herself-and-the-dead-child, and he begs or threatens—reasons with her as best he can—in his attempt to get her to restore the first group, so that there will be a man-and-wife grieving over their dead child.

He goes on: "I'm not so much / Unlike other folks as your standing there / Apart would make me out." The "standing there / Apart" is an imitative, expressive form that makes her apart, shows her apart. Really her apartness makes him out *like* other folks, all those others who make pretense of following to the grave, but who before one's back is turned have made their way back to life; but he necessarily misunderstands her, since for him being like others is necessarily good, being unlike them necessarily bad. His "Give me my chance"—he doesn't say *a* chance—reminds one of those masculine things fairness and sportsmanship, and makes one think of the child's demand for justice, equal shares, which follows his original demand for exclusive possession, the lion's share. "Give me my chance" means: "You, like everybody else, must admit that anybody deserves a chance—so give me mine"; he deserves his chance not by any particular qualities, personal merit, but just by virtue of being a human being. His "I do think, though, you overdo it a little" says that he is forced against his will to criticize her for so much exceeding (the phrase "a little" is understatement, politeness, and caution) the norm of grief, for mourning more than is usual or reasonable; the phrase "overdo it a little" manages to reduce her grief to the level of a petty social blunder. His next words, "What was it brought you up to think it the thing / To take your mother-loss of a first child / So inconsolably—in the face of love," manage to crowd four or five kinds of condemnation into a single sentence. "What was it brought you up" says that it is not your essential being but your accidental upbringing that has made you do this—it reduces the woman to a helpless social effect. "To think it the thing" is particularly insulting because it makes her grief a mere matter of fashion; it is as though he were saying, "What was it brought you up to think it the thing / To wear your skirt that far above your knees?" The phrase "to take your mother-loss of a first child" pigeonholes her loss, makes it a regular, predictable category that demands a regular, predictable amount of grief, and no more. The phrase "so inconsolably—in the face of love" condemns her for being so unreasonable as not to be consoled by, for paying no attention to, that unarguably good, absolutely general thing, love; the generalized *love* makes demands upon her that are inescapable, compared to those which would be made by a more specific phrase like "in the face of my love for you." The man's "You'd think his memory might be satisfied" again condemns her for exceeding the reasonable social norm of grief; condemns her, jealously, for mourning as if the dead child's demands for grief were insatiable.

Her interruption, "There you go sneering now!" implies that he has often before done what she calls "sneering" at her and her excessive sensitivity; and, conscious of how hard he has been trying to make peace, and unconscious of how much his words have gone over into attack, he contradicts her like a child, in righteous anger: "I'm not, I'm not!" His "You make me angry" is another of his rhetorical, tautological announcements about himself, one that is intended somehow to justify the breaking of his promise not to come down to her; he immediately makes the simple childish threat, "I'll come down to you"— he is repeating his promise, "I won't come down to you," with the "not" removed. "God, what a woman!" righteously and despairingly calls on God and public opinion (that voice of the people which is the voice of God) to witness and marvel at what he is being forced to put up with: the fantastic, the almost unbelievable wrongness and unreasonableness of this woman.

" And it's come to this," that regular piece of rhetorical recrimina-
tion in quarrels, introduces his *third* use of the sentence " Can't
a man speak of his own child he's lost"; but this time the
rhetorical question is changed into the factual condemnation
of "A man can't speak of his own child that's dead." This
time he doesn't end the sentence with the more sentimental,
decorous, sympathy-demanding "that's lost," but ends with the
categorical "that's dead."

Earlier the woman has given two entirely different, entirely
specific and unexpected answers to this rhetorical question of
his; this time she has a third specific answer, which she makes
with monosyllabic precision and finality: "You can't because
you don't know how to speak." He has said that it is an awful
thing not to be permitted to speak of his own dead child; she
replies that it is not a question of permission but of ability, that
he is too ignorant and insensitive to be *able* to speak of his
child. Her sentence is one line long, and it is only the second
sentence of hers that has been that long. He has talked at
length during the first two-thirds of the poem, she in three-
or four-word phrases or in motions without words; for the rest
of the poem she talks at length, as everything that has been
shut up inside her begins to pour out. She opens herself up,
now—is far closer to him, striking at him with her words, than
she has been sitting apart, in her place. His open attack has
finally elicited from her, by contagion, her open anger, so that
now he is something real and unbearable to attack, instead of
being something less-than-human to be disregarded.

This first sentence has indicted him; now she brings in the
specific evidence for the indictment. She says: " If you had any
feelings, you that dug / With your own hand "—but after the
three stabbing, indicting stresses of

$$\overset{/}{\text{your}} \ \overset{/}{\text{own}} \ \overset{/}{\text{hand}}$$

she breaks off the sentence, as if she found the end unbearable
to go on to; interjects, her throat tightening, the incredulous
rhetorical question, "how could you?"—and finishes with the
fact that she tries to make more nearly endurable, more euphemistic, with the tender word "little": "his little grave." The
syntax of the sentence doesn't continue, but the fact of things
continues; she says, "I saw you from that very window there."

That very window there

has the same stabbing stresses, the same emphasis on a specific,
damning actuality, that

your own hand

had—and that, soon,

my own eyes

and

your own baby's grave

and other such phrases will have. She goes on: "Making the
gravel leap and leap in air, / Leap up, like that, like that, and
land so lightly / And roll back down the mound beside the hole."
As the sentence imitates with such terrible life and accuracy the
motion of the gravel, her throat tightens and aches in her
hysterical repetition of "like that, like that": the sounds of
"leap and leap in air, / Leap up like that, like that, and land
so lightly" are "le! le! le! li! li! la! li!" and re-create the sustained
hysteria she felt as she first watched; inanimate things, the very
stones, leap and leap in air, or when their motion subsides land
"so lightly," while the animate being, her dead child, does not
move, will never move. (The foxes have holes, and the birds of
the air have nests; but the Son of man hath not where to lay his
head.) Her words "leap and leap in air, leap up, like that, like

that" keep the stones alive! alive! alive!—in the words "and land" they start to die away, but the following words "so lightly" make them alive again, for a last moment of unbearable contradiction, before they "*roll* back *down* the *mound* beside the *hole*." The repeated *o*'s (the line says "oh! ow! ow! oh!") make almost crudely actual the abyss of death into which the pieces of gravel and her child fall, not to rise again. The word "hole" (insisted on even more by the rhyme with "roll") gives to the grave the obscene actuality that watching the digging forced it to have for her.

She says: "I thought, Who is that man? I didn't know you." She sees the strange new meaning in his face (what, underneath, the face has meant all along) so powerfully that the face itself seems a stranger's. If her own husband can do something so impossibly alien to all her expectations, he has never really been anything but alien; all her repressed antagonistic knowledge about his insensitivity comes to the surface and masks what before had masked it. In the next sentence, "And I crept down the stairs and up the stairs / To look again," the word "crept" makes her a little mouselike thing crushed under the weight of her new knowledge. But the truly extraordinary word is the "and" that joins "down the stairs" to "up the stairs." What is so extraordinary is that she sees nothing extraordinary about it: the "and" joining the two co-ordinates hides from her, shows that she has repressed, the thoroughly illogical, contradictory nature of her action; it is like saying: "And I ran out of the fire and back into the fire," and seeing nothing strange about the sentence.

Her next words, "And still your spade kept lifting," give the man's tool a dead, mechanical life of its own; it keeps on and on, crudely, remorselessly, neither guided nor halted by spirit. She continues: "Then you came in. I heard your rumbling voice /

Out in the kitchen"; the word "rumbling" gives this great blind creature an insensate weight and strength that are, somehow, hollow. Then she says that she did something as extraordinary as going back up the stairs, but she masks it, this time, with the phrase "and I don't know why." She doesn't know why, it's unaccountable, "But I went near to see with my own eyes." Her "I don't know why" shows her regular refusal to admit things like these; she manages by a confession of ignorance not to have to make the connections, consciously, that she has already made unconsciously.

She now says a sentence that is an extraordinarily conclusive condemnation of him: "You could sit there with the stains on your shoes / Of the fresh earth from your own baby's grave / And talk about your everyday concerns." The five hissing or spitting s's in the strongly accented "sit," "stains," "shoes"; the whole turning upsidedown of the first line, with four trochaic feet followed by one poor iamb; the concentration of intense, damning stresses in

$$\text{fresh éarth of your ówn báby's gráve}$$

—all these things give an awful finality to the judge's summingup, so that in the last line, "and talk about your everyday concerns," the criminal's matter-of-fact obliviousness has the perversity of absolute insensitivity: Judas sits under the cross matching pennies with the soldiers. The poem has brought to life an unthought-of literal meaning of its title: this is home burial with a vengeance, burial *in* the home; the fresh dirt of the grave stains her husband's shoes and her kitchen floor, and the dirty spade with which he dug the grave stands there in the entry. As a final unnecessary piece of evidence, a last straw that comes long after the camel's back is broken, she states: "You had stood the spade up against the wall / Outside there in the entry, for I saw it." All her pieces of evidence have written underneath them, like Goya's drawing, that triumphant, traumatic, unarguable I SAW IT.

The man's next sentence is a kind of summing-up-in-little of his regular behavior, the ways in which (we have come to see) he *has* to respond. He has begged her to let him into her grief, to tell him about it if it's something human; now she lets him into not her grief but her revolted, hating condemnation of him; she does tell him about it and it isn't human, but a nightmare into which he is about to fall. He says: "I shall laugh the worst laugh I ever laughed. / I'm cursed. God, if I don't believe I'm cursed." The sounds have the gasping hollowness of some-body hit in the stomach and trying over and over to get his breath—of someone nauseated and beginning to vomit: the first stressed vowel sounds are "agh! uh! agh! uh! agh! uh!" He doesn't reply to her, argue with her, address her at all, but makes a kind of dramatic speech that will exhibit him in a role public opinion will surely sympathize with, just as he sympathizes with himself. As always, he repeats: "laugh," "laugh," and "laugh," "I'm cursed" and "I'm cursed" (the rhyme with "worst" gives almost the effect of another repetition); as always, he announces beforehand what he is going to do, rhetorically appealing to mankind for justification and sympathy. His "I shall laugh the worst laugh I ever laughed" has the queer effect of seeming almost to be quoting some folk proverb. His "I'm cursed" manages to find a category of understanding in which to pigeonhole this nightmare, makes him a reasonable human being helpless against the inhuman powers of evil—the cursed one is not to blame. His "God, if I don't believe I'm cursed" is akin to his earlier "God, what a woman!"—both have some-thing of the male's outraged, incredulous, despairing response to the unreasonableness and immorality of the female. He responds hardly at all to the exact situation; instead he demands sympathy for, sympathizes with himself for, the impossibly unlucky pigeon-hole into which Fate has dropped him.

His wife then repeats the sentence that, for her, sums up everything: "I can repeat the very words you were saying. / 'Three foggy mornings and one rainy day / Will rot the best birch fence a man can build.'" We feel with a rueful smile that he has lived by proverbs and—now, for her—dies by them. He has handled his fresh grief by making it a part of man's regular routine, man's regular work; and by quoting man's regular wisdom, that explains, explains away, pigeonholes, anything. Nature tramples down man's work, the new fence rots, but man still is victorious, in the secure summing-up of the proverb.

The bést bírch fénce

is, so far as its stresses are concerned, a firm, comfortable parody of all those stabbing stress-systems of hers. In his statement, as usual, it is not *I* but *a man*. There is a resigned but complacent, almost relishing wit about this summing-up of the transitoriness of human effort: to understand your defeat so firmly, so pro-verbially, is in a sense to triumph. He has seen his ordinary human ambition about that ordinary human thing, a child, frus-trated by death; so there is a certain resignation and pathos about his saying what he says. The word "rot" makes the con-nection between the fence and the child, and it is the word "rot" that is unendurable to the woman, since it implies with obscene directness: how many foggy mornings and rainy days will it take to rot the best flesh-and-blood child a man can have? Just as, long ago at the beginning of the poem, the man brought the bedroom and the grave together, he brings the rotting child and the rotting fence together now. She says in incredulous,

breathless outrage: "Think of it, talk like that at such a time!"
(The repeated sounds, *th*, *t*, *t*, *th*, *t*, *t*, are thoroughly expressive.)
But once more she has repressed the connection between the two
things: she objects to the sentence not as what she knows it is,
as rawly and tactlessly relevant, but as something absolutely
irrelevant, saying: "What had how long it takes a birch to rot /
To do with"—and then she puts in a euphemistic circumlocution,
lowers her eyes and lowers the shades so as not to see—"what
was in the darkened parlor."

But it is time to go back and think of just what it was the
woman saw, just how she saw it, to make her keep on repeating
that first occasion of its sight. She saw it on a holy and awful
day. The child's death and burial were a great and almost
unendurable occasion, something that needed to be accompanied
with prayer and abstention, with real grief and the ritual expression of grief. It was a holy or holi-day that could only be dese-
crated by "everyday concerns"; the husband's digging seemed
to the wife a kind of brutally unfeeling, secular profanation of
that holy day, her holy grief. Her description makes it plain
that her husband dug strongly and well. And why should he
not do so? Grief and grave-digging, for him, are in separate
compartments; the right amount of grief will never flow over
into the next compartment. To him it is the workaday, matter-
of-fact thing that necessarily comes first; grieving for the corpse
is no excuse for not having plenty of food at the wake. If
someone had said to him: "You dig mighty well for a man that's
just lost his child," wouldn't he have replied: "Grief's no reason
for doing a bad job"? (And yet, the muscles tell the truth; a
sad enough man shovels badly.) When, the grave dug and the
spade stood up in the entry, he went into the kitchen, he may
very well have felt: "A good job," just as Yakov, in *Rothschild's
Fiddle*, taps the coffin he has made for his wife and thinks:
"A good job."

But unconsciously, his wife has far more compelling reasons to be appalled at this job her husband is doing. Let me make this plain. If we are told how a woman dreams of climbing the stairs, and of looking out through a window at a man digging a hole with a spade—digging powerfully, so that the gravel leaps and leaps into the air, only to roll back down into the hole; and still the man's spade keeps lifting and plunging down, lifting and plunging down, as she watches in fascinated horror, creeps down the stairs, creeps back up against her will, to keep on watching; and then, she doesn't know why, she has to go to see with her own eyes the fresh earth staining the man's shoes, has to see with her own eyes the man's tool stood up against the wall, in the entrance to the house—if we are told such a dream, is there any doubt what *sort* of dream it will seem to us? Such things have a sexual force, a sexual meaning, as much in our waking hours as in our dreams—as we know from how many turns of speech, religious rites, myths, tales, works of art. When the plowman digs his plow into the earth, Mother Earth, to make her bear, this does not have a sexual appropriateness only in the dreams of neurotic patients—it is something that we all understand, whether or not we admit that we understand. So the woman understood her husband's digging. If the spade, the tool that he stands up in the entry, stands for man's workaday world, his matter-of-fact objectivity and disregard of emotion, it also stands for his masculinity, his sexual power; on this holy day he brings back into the house of grief the soiling stains of fresh earth, of this digging that, to her, is more than digging.

That day of the funeral the grieving woman felt only misery and anguish, passive suffering; there was nobody to blame for it all except herself. And how often women do blame themselves for the abnormality or death of a baby! An old doctor says: they keep blaming themselves; they should have done this, that, something; they forget all about their husbands; often they blame some doctor who, by not coming immediately, by doing or not doing something, was responsible for it all: the woman's feeling of guilt about other things is displaced onto the child's death. Now when this woman sees her husband digging the grave (doing what seems to her, consciously, an intolerably insensitive thing; unconsciously, an indecent thing) she *does* have someone to blame, someone upon whom to shift her own guilt: she is able to substitute for passive suffering and guilt an active loathing and condemnation—as she blames the man's greater guilt and wrongness her own lesser guilt can seem in comparison innocence and rightness. (The whole matrix of attitudes available to her, about woman as Madonna-and-child and man as brute beast, about sexuality as a defiling thing forced upon woman, helps her to make this shift.) The poem has made it easy for us to suspect a partial antagonism or uncongeniality, sexually, between the weak oversensitive woman and the strong insensitive man, with his sexual force so easily transformed into menace. (The poem always treats it in that form.) The woman's negative attitudes have been overwhelmingly strengthened, now; it is plain that since the child's death there has been no sort of sexual or emotional union between them.

To her, underneath, the child's death must have seemed a punishment. Of whom for what? Of them for what they have done—sexual things are always tinged with guilt; but now her complete grief, her separateness and sexual and emotional abstention, help to cancel out her own guilt—the man's matter-of-fact physical obliviousness, his desire to have everything what it was before, reinforce his own guilt and help to make it seem absolute. Yet, underneath, the woman's emotional and physiological needs remain unchanged, and are satisfied by this compulsory symptomatic action of hers—this creeping up the stairs, looking, looking, creeping down and then back up again, looking, looking; she stares with repudiating horror, with accepting fascination, at this obscenely symbolic sight. It is not the child's mound she stares at, but the scene of the crime, the site of this terrible symbolic act that links sexuality and death, the marriage-bed and the grave. (Afterward she had gone down into the kitchen to see the man flushed and healthy, breathing a little harder after physical exertion; her words, "I heard your *rumbling* voice out in the kitchen," remind us of that first telling description of him on the stairs, "*mounting* until she *cowered* under him." Her first response to the sight, "I thought: Who *is* that man? I didn't know you," makes him not her husband but a stranger, a guilty one, whom she is right to remain estranged from, must remain estranged from.) Her repeated symptomatic act has the consciousness of obsessional-compulsive symptoms, not the unconsciousness of hysterical blindness or paralysis: she is conscious of what she is doing, knows how it all began; and yet she cannot keep from doing it, does not really know why she does it, and is conscious only of a part of the meaning it has for her. She has isolated it, and refuses to see its connections, consciously, because the connections are so powerful unconsciously: so that she says, "And I crept down the stairs *and* up the stairs"; says, "*And I don't know why,* / But I went near to see with my own eyes"; says, "What had how long it takes a birch to rot / To do with what was in the darkened parlor?"

This repeated symptomatic action of hers satisfies several needs. It keeps reassuring her that she is right to keep herself fixed in separation and rejection. By continually revisiting this scene, by looking again and again at—so to speak—this indecent photograph of her husband's crime, she is making certain that she will never come to terms with the criminal who, in the photograph, is committing the crime. Yet, underneath, there is a part of her that takes guilty pleasure in the crime, that is in identifying complicity with the criminal. A symptom or symptomatic action is an expression not only of the defense against the forbidden wish, but also of the forbidden wish.

If the reader doubts that this symptomatic action of hers has a sexual root, he can demonstrate it to himself by imagining the situation different in one way. Suppose the wife had looked out of the window and seen her husband animatedly and matter-of-factly bargaining to buy a cemetery lot from one of the next day's funeral guests. She would have been angered and revolted. But would she have crept back to look again? have gone into the kitchen so as to see the bargainer with her own eyes? have stared in fascination at the wallet from which he had taken the money? Could she as easily have made a symptom of it?

After she has finished telling the story of what she had seen, of what he had done, she cries: "You *couldn't* care!" The words say: "If you could behave as you behaved it proves that you didn't care and, therefore, that you couldn't care; if you, my own husband, the child's own father, were unable to care, it proves that it must be impossible for anyone to care." So she goes on, not about him but about everyone: "The nearest friends can go / With anyone to death, comes so far short / They might as well not try to go at all." The sentence has some of the rueful, excessive wit of Luther's "In every good act the just man sins"; man can do so little he might as well do nothing. Her next sentence, "No, from the time when one is sick to death, / One is alone, and he dies more alone," tolls like a lonely bell for the human being who grieves for death and, infected by what she grieves for, dies alone in the pest house, deserted by the humanity that takes good care not to be infected. When you truly feel what death is, you must die: all her phrases about the child's death and burial make them her own death and burial.

She goes on: "Friends make pretence of following to the grave, / But before one is in it their minds are turned"—her "make pretence" blames their, his, well-meant hypocrisy; her "before one is in it" speaks of the indecent haste with which he hurried to dig the grave into which the baby was put, depriving her of it—of the indecent haste with which he forgot death and wanted to resume life. The phrases "their minds are turned" and "making the best of their way back" are (as so often with Frost) queerly effective adaptations of ordinary idioms, of "their backs are turned" and "making the best of things"; these are the plain roots, in the woman's mind, of her less direct and more elaborate phrases. But when we have heard her whole sentence: "Friends make pretense of following to the grave / But before one is in it their minds are turned / And making the best of their way back to life / And living people, and things they understand," we reply: "As they must." She states as an evil what we think at worst a necessary evil; she is condemning people for not committing suicide, for not going down into the grave with the corpse and dying there. She condemns the way of the world, but it is the way of any world that continues to be a world: the world that does otherwise perishes. Her "But the world's evil. I won't have grief so / If I can change it. Oh, I won't, I won't!" admits what grief is to everybody else; is generally; and says that she will change the universal into her own contradictory particular if she can: the sentence has its own defeat inside it. What this grieving woman says about grief is analogous to a dying woman's saying about death: "I won't have death so / If I can change it. Oh, I won't, I won't!" Even the man responds to the despairing helplessness in her "Oh, I won't, I won't!" She is still trying to be faithful and unchanging in her grief, but already she has begun to be faithless, has begun to change. Saying, "I never have colds any more," an hour or two before one has a cold, is one's first unconscious recognition that one has caught cold; similarly, she says that other people forget and change but that she never will, just when she has begun to change—just when, by telling her husband the cause of her complete separation, she has begun to destroy the completeness of the separation. Her "Oh, I won't, I won't!" sounds helplessly dissolving, running-down; already contains within it the admission of what it denies. Her "I won't have grief so" reminds us that grief *is* so, is by its very nature a transition to something that isn't grief. She knows it too, so that she says that everybody else is that way, the world is that way, but they're wrong, they're evil; *someone* must be different; *someone* honorably and quixotically, at no matter what cost, must contradict the nature of grief, the nature of the world.

All this is inconceivable to the man: if everybody is that way, it must be right to be that way; it would be insanity to think of any other possibility. She has put grief, the dead child, apart on an altar, to be kept separate and essential as long as possible—forever, if possible. He has immediately filed away the child, grief, in the pigeonhole of man's wont, man's proverbial understanding: the weight is off his own separate shoulders, and the shoulders of all mankind bear the burden. In this disaster of her child's death, her husband's crime, her one consolation is that she is inconsolable, has (good sensitive woman) grieved for months as her husband (bad insensitive man) was not able to grieve even for hours. Ceasing to grieve would destroy this consolation, would destroy the only way of life she has managed to find.

And yet she has begun to destroy them. When she says at the end of the poem: "How can I make you—" understand, see, she shows in her baffled, longing despair that she *has* tried to make him understand; has tried to help him as he asked her to help him. Her "You *couldn't* care," all her lines about what friends and the world necessarily are, excuse him in a way, by making him a necessarily insensitive part of a necessarily insensitive world that she alone is sensitive in: she is the one person desperately and forlornly trying to be different from everyone else, as she tries to keep death and grief alive in the middle of a world intent on its own forgetful life. At these last moments she does not, as he thinks, "set him apart" as "so much unlike other folks"; if he could hear and respond to what she actually has said, there would be some hope for them. But he doesn't; instead of understanding her special situation, he dumps her into the pigeonhole of the crying woman—any crying woman—and then tries to *manage* her as one manages a child. She does try to let him into her grief, but he won't go; instead he tells her that now she's had her cry, that now she feels better, that the heart's gone out of it, that there's really no grief left for him to be let into.

The helpless tears into which her hard self-righteous separateness has dissolved show, underneath, a willingness to accept understanding; she has denounced him, made a clean breast of things, and now is accessible to the understanding or empathy that he is unable to give her. Women are oversensitive, exaggerate everything, tell all, weep, and then are all right: this is the pigeonhole into which he drops her. So rapid an understanding can almost be called a form of stupidity, of not even trying really to understand. The bewitched, uncanny, almost nauseated helplessness of what he has said a few lines before: "I shall laugh the worst laugh I ever laughed. / I'm cursed. God, if I don't believe I'm cursed," has already changed into a feeling of mastery, of the strong man understanding and managing the weak hysterical woman. He is the powerful one now. His " There, you have said it all and you feel better. You won't go now," has all the grownup's condescension toward the child, the grownup's ability to make the child do something simply by stating that the child is about to do it. The man's " You're crying. Close the door. / The heart's gone out of it: why keep it up," shows this quite as strikingly; he feels that he can manipulate her back into the house and into his life, back out of the grief that— he thinks or hopes—no longer has any heart in it, so that she must pettily and exhaustingly " keep it up."

But at this moment when the depths have been opened for him; at this moment when the proper management might get her back into the house, the proper understanding get her back into his life; at this moment that it is fair to call the most important moment of his life, someone happens to come down the road. Someone who will see her crying and hatless in the doorway; someone who will go back to the village and tell everything; someone who will shame them in the eyes of the world. Public opinion, what people will say, is more important to him than anything she will do; he forgets everything else, and expostulates: " Amy! There's someone coming down the road! " His exclamation is full of the tense, hurried fear of social impropriety, of public disgrace; nothing could show more forcibly what he *is* able to understand, what he *does* think of primary importance. Her earlier " Oh, where's my hat? Oh, I don't need it! " prepares for, is the exact opposite of, his " Amy! There's someone coming down the road! "

She says with incredulous, absolute intensity and particularity: " *You—*"

That italicized *you* is the worst, the most nearly final thing that she can say about him, since it merely points to what he is. She doesn't go on; goes back and replies to his earlier sentences: "oh, you think the talk is all." Her words have a despairing limpness and sadness: there is no possibility of his being made to think anything different, to see the truth under the talk. She says: "I must go—" and her words merely recognize a reality—"Somewhere out of this house." Her final words are full of a longing, despairing, regretful realization of a kind of final impossibility: "How can I make you—" The word that isn't said, that she stops short of saying, is as much there as anything in the poem. All her insistent anxious pride in her own separateness and sensitiveness and superiority is gone; she knows, now, that she is separate from him no matter what she wants. Her "How can I make you—" amounts almost to: "If only I could make you—if only there were some way to make you—but there is no way."

He responds not to what she says but to what she does, to "She was opening the door wider." He threatens, as a child would threaten: "If—you—do!" He sounds like a giant child, or a child being a giant or an ogre. The "If—you—do!" uses as its principle of being the exaggerated slowness and heaviness, the *willedness* of his nature. (Much about him reminds me of Yeats' famous definition: "Rhetoric is the will trying to do the work of the imagination"; "Home Burial" might be called the story of a marriage between the will and the imagination.) The dashes Frost inserts between the words slow down the words to the point where the slowedness or heaviness itself, as pure force and menace, is what is communicated. Then the man says, trying desperately—feebly—to keep her within reach of that force or menace: "Where do you mean to go? First tell me that. / I'll follow and bring you back by force. I *will!*" The last sentences of each of her previous speeches (her despairing emotional "Oh, I won't! I won't!" and her despairing spiritual "How can I make you—") are almost the exact opposite of the "I *will!*"

with which he ends the poem. It is appropriate that "force," "I," and "*will*" are his last three words: his proverbial, town-meeting understanding has failed, just as his blankly imploring humility has failed; so that he has to resort to the only thing he has left, the will or force that seems almost like the mass or inertia of a physical body. We say that someone "throws his weight around," and in the end there is nothing left for him to do but throw his weight around. Appropriately, his last line is one more rhetorical announcement of what he is going to do: he will follow and bring her back by force; and, appropriately, he ends the poem with one more repetition—he repeats: "I *will!*"

Author Index